THE SPORT COACH

The PSYCHOLOGY behind coaching

JANNIE PUTTER

First Edition, 2016
ISBN: 978-1-77605-277-6
e-ISBN: 978-1-77605-275-2

Published by Kwarts Publishers
www.kwarts.co.za

With gratitude

To my amazing parents..
And every teacher and coach
who touched and shaped me
into who I am today...

CONTENTS

FOREWORD

Sport is an enormous industry! The influence of competition, sport stars, heroes and legends on how society acts, what we speak about, what we believe, what we hope and what we buy is constantly becoming more significant and meaningful.

The things our children dream about – becoming champions, being people of influence, to be significant in history, is what fills our daily conversations. The potential wealth and fame present in becoming a sport star has caused a movement of interest, commitment and dedication towards mastering sporting skills amongst people of all classes and all races. The sport stars in our world influence nations, society, cultures as well as the world's economy. History books are written about these people and their stories...

Many things happen daily – leaders fall and leaders rise. Wars starts and wars end. There are numerous international talent competitions taking place – almost daily. There are people who move and shock the world with their incredible abilities. There are magicians performing unimaginable things, yet we will all agree that the event which has the biggest influence on humanity and society is surely the Olympic Games - a sporting event which takes place every four years with the aim of determining the world's best. Every country in the world hopes to have an athlete representing them at this global sporting event. The performances of a single athlete can change a whole nation's moral and social atmosphere. Sport influences society in major ways.

World champions become the heroes of their time. Their stories become the fantasies of our children's children. Their lives and accomplishments become the inspiration of our youth. Their influence on society is majestic. What they do, influence the wealthiest people on our planet. The sport stars determine trends. They set standards. People use their lives as examples of influence and inspiration because these champions are people just like you and me – normal people who simply do more than the average person is willing to do. They go beyond the average. They do this by making quality decisions and extreme commitments in their own lives...

What these champions have in common is a very significant, yet almost unnoticeable factor. Each of these champions has a coach. Someone who influences their life-choices, their core beliefs and their daily behaviour. We look at these champions with huge admiration and respect, yet behind them there are always a team of people... because no-one ever makes it to the top alone!

This book is for and about everyone influencing the life of another – whether you are a teacher, a sport coach, a mentor or a parent – you are a coach in some or other way! Coaches are seldom seen as heroes. From time to time their influence and their roles are acknowledged by a society craving for heroes!

Coaches are people who not only influence and change the lives of the champions of the world. Coaches are people who influence the lives of the majority of people on this planet. Everyone reading this book can testify to the influence a coach had on you in some stage in your life. On your self-image, your dreams and your level of motivation! We all know that a coach has the power to nurture your dream or to kill your dream! Coaches are people who can make or break you! Not necessarily into a world champion, but definitely into a better and fuller you!

In my own life I can testify about the significant role each coach I had played! Some of them made me strong. Others lost me and others broke me. I was like clay in their hands. Looking back I often wonder:

"What could have happened if they knew what I was willing to do for them?" I sometimes wish they had expected more of me. I wish they believed in me more... I needed that! On the other hand I also see those coaches who saw more in me than I believed myself. They expected more of me than I believed possible. I stand amazed. They were all right! I was like clay: ready to be moulded into whoever *they thought* I could be!

I look at the masses of young children, all of them dreaming of becoming super-stars, heroes and legends! All of them (as well as their parents) fantasize about the wealth and fame of being a champion. People do whatever they can to achieve this. They buy the best equipment, they travel around the world, they read the books of champions, and they try to find the best coaches. They do everything possible to become front-runners in this race towards fame.

We often tend to forget about the most important role player in this process - the coach! Who teaches the coach? Who counsels him? Do we really know who they are? How does one become a coach – a total coach and not simply a specialist in one or two fields? What are the steps in the process of becoming a coach and a mentor who can literally make or break the life of another human being? How do you become someone who unlocks the potential in another person instead of simply using (and abusing) who they are?

Looking at coaches, I realise most of them do not understand how much power they truly have! Most coaches don't know that they can create belief, confidence, hopes and self-esteem in the athletes they work with. Too many coaches are blinded by the pressures of the system (parents, schools, administrators, politicians, sponsors etc.) to deliver results (winning) at the cost of the lives (their physical development, their self-esteem, their hopes and their beliefs) of the people they work with. The result hereof is paramount in the shocking statistics which shows that about 3 out of 4 children who take part in sport at primary school level will stop their involvement with sport when they go to high-school.

Their personal disappointments, their disappointed parents, their negative experiences, their broken spirits and the risk of ridicule they face sometimes just becomes too much. The safest place is the spectator stands. From there they can look, envy and criticize those few who are willing to take the risks involved in living a dream. Too many lives are ruined because we (society) pressure our young children into becoming responsible adults before they are ready to understand the demands, the responsibilities and sacrifices involved in becoming true champions. Too many children become burn-outs in this race towards fame!

Yes, there are inspiring stories of total coaches – people who do more than coaching a technique and correcting mistakes. People who know that building a true champion is much more than simply teaching a technique and a skill. People who know that it takes much more than a temporary victory on the score-board to become a true champion. People who understand that to be a true champion is not only meas-ured by a result. It is a never-ending process of commitment, sacrifices, moments of joy as well as moments of defeat! Most significant about the road to glory is the challenges the champions master in the process of getting there! *Coaching is the journey* you take *with* someone else. It is about assisting another person to discover, develop, overcome and master the challenges and skills necessary to become the best he / she can be. Success is a constant endeavour – not a destination which you reach.

The end-goal of coaching is to become a total coach. To be significant in assisting, building and maintaining true champions. True coaching is about one's ability to guide and assist someone in becoming a master in both a particular sport as well as in life. Some of those you work with might even become world champions in their specific sports! Some might just become far more than they ever would have been, had it not been for your influence. The truth is that no coach really knows whom they are working with...

The world gives glory and acknowledges those sport stars who break records and set new standards. The acknowledgement and glory goes to the athlete – not to the coach! The reward of a coach is to witness and enjoy the glory of his / her athletes. The biggest reward life really has to offer is to know that you have made a positive difference in the lives of other people. That is where the real reward of coaching comes alive! Not only in creating champions on the sporting field, but making a difference in creating more complete and more disciplined individuals who might simply become better parents, employers, employees or politicians for that matter! It is about planting and nurturing a seed of excellence and commitment in every person you coach!

> *You will have everything you can dream of in life, if you can help enough other people achieve their dreams...*
>
> - Zig Ziglar

1.

WHY WOULD YOU BECOME A COACH?

WHAT IS YOUR REASON FOR COACHING?

○ Were you perhaps one of those few who had the talent and commitment, yet the moment of opportunity slipped by because you were not ready when it arrived? Perhaps this missed opportunity inspired you to impart your experience to make sure that it is not missed by another because of ignorance or arrogance... Your time has passed, but the mistakes you made prepared you for the journey you can now take with someone else!

○ Do you perhaps have a calling in your life to motivate, inspire and assist others in developing their talents to their full potential?

○ Does it perhaps give you a deep personal joy when you are instrumental in helping someone else achieve great accomplishments?

○ Do you perhaps have exciting and inspiring dreams about amazing achievements, yet it is only possible through the physical abilities of others (whom you guide and assist) because you yourself are limited in your own physical abilities?

- o Do you perhaps dream of the wealth and fame hidden in the opportunity of coaching someone else to become a true champion?

- o It might be that the financial rewards associated with successfully coaching and training someone to become a world-class athlete is a huge factor in your decision to start this journey?

- o Perhaps you yourself were coached by someone who brought out the best in you in a special way and you want to continue this deed? Or were you perhaps coached by someone who did not know how to bring out the best in you and you want to do it differently?

- o Perhaps you are someone with a passion for children and their potential and achievements. Perhaps your gift is not in performing but in coaching. Perhaps your aim is not so much the achievements that are recognised by this world but rather knowing that you made a positive impact in the lives of many young children who needed someone to guide them to stand up in life. Fame and glory is not your aim, but rather development and growth!

I am sure that your reason for coaching is known to you. Every one of us has a reason for doing what we do. My reason for writing this book is to impact and inspire those of you who coach in a positive way so that the people whose lives you touch will be better, stronger and more meaningful in themselves. Your reason will determine how you are going to tackle this adventure of coaching. Maybe you will do what is necessary and acceptable. Maybe you will do more. Who knows what you might accomplish?

2.

WHAT DETERMINES THE SUCCESS OF COACHING?

✓ Is it the win-loss records of your athletes?

✓ Is it the immeasurable impact you have on people's lives?

✓ Is it your ability to get someone with average ability to perform at an excellent level?

✓ Is it your ability to inspire and ignite a belief in others to do what they really only dreamed of?

✓ Is it your ability to give people with average talent an experience of true success even thought they might not be crowned as champions?

✓ Is it your ability to identify talent and to develop that talent into becoming a true champion?

✓ Is it perhaps your wisdom to understand whom you are working with? Is it your ability to create a team and do things with people they would never have done on their own?

✓ Is it your ability to facilitate and manage a group of diverse individuals into becoming a masterful team?

✓ Is it your ability to identify strengths and then to develop strengths into masterful skills?

Success in coaching might be measured and evaluated in a variety of ways. *Success is a perception – not an absolute truth!* The answer to this question is therefore not that simple… Your answer is not the same as mine or anyone else. Your answer is in you! May you achieve your dream and goal. May you live a life of being significant on this planet in the time that you are here!

3.

WHAT IS THE ROLE OF THE COACH?

As we all know, children from the same home with the same circum-stances and the same upbringing will differ dramatically. We are all unique and different. As a coach you have to know that no athlete you work with is like another. Everyone is unique! People differ inherent – in their DNA (their mind and spirit). Only a fool will think that he can treat different individuals in the same way and hope to be successful in coaching them. The key to successfully working with human beings lies in **wisdom**. The wisdom to know **what to do with whom and when to do it**! Coaching is not about you – it is all about the child or athlete or team you work with.

The goal of parenting is to inspire (show), empower (give opportuni-ties) and mentor (coach) your child in hitting his / her mark in life (live a meaningful and purposeful life).

The goal of coaching is to understand whom you are working with and then to inspire and empower that individual or team to achieve their full potential. The aim of coaching is not to become a person of such importance that you have a manipulating power over the talents and abilities of the athletes you work with. Such a coach will have athletes who are dependent upon him / her. They will be unable to make decisions for themselves. You might feel powerful, but you are not. If you are surrounded by weak (insecure) people it means you are weak yourself!

The aim of coaching is to optimize the ability of the athletes you work with which will enable them to perform skills, make correct decisions (in the heat of the moment), express a willingness to take risks and trust themselves in performing particular tasks or challenges. Thereby they will live exciting, daring, adventurous and meaningful lives and who knows – they might even become the next world champion!

The fame and glory of the moment will go to the athlete(s). Part of that glory and fame will come to you. You should always be in the shade-side of the fame and glory of the moment! Coaching is serving! That is how it should be. It is part of the mystery of being a real coach. It should never be about you – it should always be about your athlete / team!

The search for real coaches has become so intense that you (if you are truly one) will never be without opportunities. If you are truly good – people will find you! Every story of success in history has been the result of a process – never a quick fix. It might look like a quick success to the naked eye, but behind the success of every worth-while endeavour is a *process of growth*. Growth is never a quick thing. Real growth doesn't have a short-cut! Short cuts to success don't exist even though the world might want us all to think it! Short cut stories always have sad endings... The short cuts to gaining massive and bulky muscles through the injection of anabolic steroids is a great example of what I mean. Only a fool will be fooled!

You don't become a real coach overnight. You have to start your journey somewhere... You have to learn about planning, about agreements, about hope, about expectations, about disappointments, about heartaches, about excitement, about *keeping on keeping on*. All of this is part of the process of becoming a real coach!

We are all different. Our differences cause us to interpret things differently. People attach different values to the same events. Some will interpret harsh words as an indication that you are disappointed in them and that they have failed you. To others harsh words will simply mean that you see more potential in them and they need to heighten their intensity. Some people will take harsh words as a personal accusation whilst others take those same words as a source of motivation. The same words with the same intention and the same intensity – yet totally different interpretations (and results)! One athlete loses trust and his willingness to take risks (heart) whilst the other athlete flourishes and perform better. Your work as coach is to know **how** to work **with whom**! The reality is that you often don't get a second chance.

My own son lost his passion and love for the game of rugby because of his interpretation of the reactions and methods of his grade one rugby coach. The coach did not understand the youngsters and their reason for taking part in the game. He did not understand how to work with my son (and many of the other boys). He worked with them as he was – not as they were! He lost their hearts.

One of the biggest traps many coaches step into is the trap of familiarity. Many coaches who work with young children may think that the kids are too ignorant to understand a lack of knowledge and commitment. Coaches pretend to have the 'know-how' of coaching - but they don't! They thumb-suck and in many cases they try to duplicate what they have seen in a YouTube video or a television clip. The *foundational knowledge and understanding regarding specific skills* are non-existent! Most primary school coaches just do a job. They keep children busy with a few basic exercises they learned attending an elementary coaching course. Most of them try to duplicate exercises they've seen on television. ***The foundational principles are never taught because they don't know them***!

How many of us have stepped into this trap? We teach something we think we know, but the truth is we have no understanding of the underlying principles which are necessary to be successful in a skill. How many of us have worked with children without really knowing whom we worked with? Had you known that you were working with the next Springbok or the next world champion you probably would have done it differently!

Familiarity is a comfort zone and a trap many (even the best coaches) often step into. You don't coach who your athlete is, you coach who you are! You don't think about how your athlete interprets and sees things – you coach how YOU interpret and see things! It takes time to build trust. Any coach can put forth his best foot in the beginning of a coaching relationship. You give it your best to win the hearts and the trust of your athletes. Once you have it, you need to treat it gently. *Trust can be lost in a moment!* Becoming a team (coach and athlete) is essential.

Once your combination works well and performances improve, this team might need to expand. No-one ever makes it to the top alone! When a coach is mature enough and safe in himself he will expand this team by involving more specialists into the process of preparing his athlete(s) for competition. The better an athlete becomes, the bigger the need for specialist coaching and training. This means that the team will expand.

In the world of sports this team might look like this:

a) Head coach
b) Physical conditioner
c) Technical advisor
d) Specialist coaches. (In the game of rugby this means...)
   i. Scrum coach
   ii. Line-out coach
   iii. Back-line coach
   iv. Attacking coach
   v. Defence coach
   vi. Kicking coach

e) Mental coach
f) Dietician
g) Manager / administrator
h) Public relations manager / coordinator
i) Agents
j) Sponsors etc...

In the future there are going to be even more specialists in several areas. The reason: Research and development never stops! The quest to find the marginal difference-makers constantly intensifies. The rewards associated with success increase daily.

Consider the following:

a) Eye coaching
b) Hand-eye coordination coaching
c) Feet coaching (movement)
d) Core coaching (flexibility and strength)
e) Rhythm coaching
f) Judgement coaching
g) Focus coaching
h) Social media filter
i) Etc...

If you look at this list and you are older than 40 years you will probably ask the question: *"Is all this really necessary? Is this not the responsibility of the coach?"* A fact of life is: Things constantly change. *Whoever refuses to embrace change will stagnate and die*! New techniques are developed daily. New understanding of the laws of the universe causes us to improve constantly. New discoveries are made daily!

How would you have reacted to the thought that a 50-ton aeroplane will be able to take off gently into the air in the year 1950? You would have believed it to be impossible. Yet - our young generations of today think nothing of it – it is part of their lives.

Let me take you back to the legendary event performed by a man with the name Roger Bannister on the 6th of May 1954. For decades the attempt to run a mile in less than 4 minutes was futile. No-one could do it! Even medical doctors became convinced that no-one would ever be able to do it. They were so sure that they claimed that the human body won't be able to deal with the strain put on the heart in the attempt to run that fast. They went so far as to predict that the human heart would burst if it went beyond that limit.

Roger Bannister was not threatened by these predictions. In fact, he was motivated, challenged and inspired. He started to train with the aim to break the 4-minute barrier - and he did! Today it is no surprise when an athlete runs a mile in less than 4 minutes. As a matter of fact, the current world record of Hicham El Guerrouj of Morocco was set on the 7th of July 1999 and his time was a staggering 3 min, 43.13 seconds! More than 16 seconds faster than what was believed to be impossible to achieve!

Another fact is that with change (from a position of comfort and familiarity) the human mind will always offer some form of resistance. Comfort and familiarity provides a feeling of security and predictability - a safe place. In the world of coaching, doing unfamiliar things might be risky for your future (as coach) as well as the future of the athletes you work with! *"What if it does not work? What if someone gets hurt?"* You are working with someone's life and dreams! The easiest thing to do is to step back to the traditional ways and familiar methods of coaching. Technological development and our increased understanding of the physical and mental principles do not allow us to get stuck in comfort. If you want to be a front-runner in the quest to go further, faster, higher and be stronger you will have to continue growing and adapting to changes. The goal is to develop these changes ourselves! Most importantly, you will have to continue expanding your beliefs about what is possible!

BUILDING A COACHING TEAM

The most important role player in this team of coach and athlete remains you – the coach! As you believe, your athletes will believe. Only a coach can give 100% authority to any other specialist joining this team. You have to edify, sell and agree with any new specialist you bring onto this team. If your athletes have any doubts or uncertainty about another member of the coaching team it will never work! *If an athlete does not have 100% trust and belief in a coach, coaching is impossible*!

EXAMPLE:

You invite a dietician to talk and teach your athletes about correct eating-habits. Unless you had a personal meeting and discussion with this person, and unless you agree to and commit, support and edify his / her viewpoints and advice, this will be a waste of time. You *HAVE TO* believe in what this person teaches (and preaches). Only if you believe, can you expect your athletes to believe too. It can never be a nice-to-have alternative. Your athletes have to buy in. There is **NO ALTERNATIVE**. You either believe or you don't! You either commit or you quit. You (as coach) will have to **back**, **expect** and **do** exactly what that dietician discussed and taught! You are either part of the team or you are not. Many coaches get specialists to provide a nice-to-have-alternative. Little do they realise that what they really do is to open a back-door for failure!

When you ask me to become the mental coach of your athletes, you will have to agree with my philosophy (the way I approach things). If you don't, don't ask me! It will simply cause doubt and conflict in your athlete's minds and it will do more harm than good. We have to speak the same language. What it means is that you (as coach) will be accountable for every specialist's approach in the same manner as if it was you yourself coaching it to your athletes. It is a TEAM at work – even if it is eventually only one athlete performing the task. If I was to say: "*We focus our attention ONLY on finding solutions and waste no energy on speaking about the mistakes*", you will have to do exactly that in your coaching. You have to stop your athletes when you see them deviate from this agreement. You have to tell them: "*We focus only on solutions – not problems – those are what we decided in the session with Jannie*". You edify me. Now we work together as a team.

This is how a team is built! Each and every member of the team back and edify each other. We function together as a unit, speaking the same language. When one member of the team has a session with the athlete (s) the other members of the team has to know what is discussed or preferably attend the session themselves. Each member of this team has to understand the principles which are discussed and taught by any other specialist on the team. The moment one member of a team overrules another, trust is lost and a door is opened for doubt and failure!

When you decide to enlarge and strengthen the team it is imperative that you know, **agree and support** the person (specialist) and his / her methods. It is the only way you build a real team.

The dependency and loyalty your athletes have towards you (as main coach) will always cause them to seek your acknowledgement and agreement before they accept the teaching and coaching of any other specialist!

THE EMOTIONAL RESPONSIBILITIES OF A COACH:

You enter an extreme vulnerable personal scenario the moment you commit yourself to become a coach. Any athlete takes a huge risk in trusting you with their energy, their dreams, their desires and their emotions when they engage into this relationship. To commit fully an athlete needs some form of security or belief that they will be safe with you.

Creating a safe place is largely dependent upon you. You have to be willing to face all the risks with your athlete. You will risk *failure*. You will risk *embarrassment*. You will risk *ridicule*. You will risk *being lonely*. You will risk *anxiety and stress*. You will risk *sacrifices*. You will risk *rejection*. You will risk *pressure*. You will risk *expectations*. You will risk *being important and well-known*. You will risk *privacy*. You will risk *fame and wealth*. You will have to cover your athlete in every challenge he / she faces. Nobody ever makes it alone – we all need others. You will be that *other* in the life of your athlete!

Your athlete will trust you with EVERYTHING! You have to be worthy of that trust! You'll need to stand in the gap. You will largely be responsible for this relationship. You can't commit only to a part of it. It is ALL or nothing! You can't commit to only teaching a technique. Sport and competition is much more than just technique. You can't commit only to the fitness of your athletes. Sport is much more than fitness. You can't commit only to a game plan. Sport is much more than simply a game plan! If you plan to commit to only a part of it – then advertise and sell yourself as a specialist – not a coach!

Any specialist can eventually become a real coach. There are many specialists who sell themselves as coaches, yet they are merely specialists. As a specialist you will only be able to take your athletes to a certain level but that's it. To take them further you will have to get PERSONAL. You have to be willing (and able) to move into the role as mentor and a trusting friend. Throughout history certain people have achieved this goal of becoming a real coach. They became true legends! They left a legacy in the form of better people, excellent cultures and admirable principles. Many of them are not known. Many of them are the teachers in our schools. Many of them are those special parents the world does not know. The biggest challenge to becoming a real coach is probably your ability to deal correctly and sensitively with your athletes on an emotional level.

Familiarity is a trap a real coach should never step into! You have to back your athletes irrespective of human error and weaknesses. You have to know who you are working with! You have to be prepared. All athletes will reach a place of emotional weakness at some time or another. It happens in the presence of fatigue, under pressure, when fear is present and when the demands become intense. It might happen when athletes experience personal emotional challenges. It might also happen when success becomes too much.

You will often find that some athletes are not prepared or ready for the responsibilities accompanying success. To them success becomes an unconscious threat. As coach you can never take these situations personally. You need to be aware of these challenges and you have to protect your athletes in moments like these. *Success is always a process, not an event*!

You need to be the source of power in moments like these. You don't have the luxury of losing your cool! You can't fold under pressure. You are the leader of this relationship. You have to remain in control. You have to make wise decisions and provide solutions. You have to act with authority at all times. Your athlete is not the strong one in situations like these, you are! Take responsibility for it and guide your athletes through it.

Every athlete has a responsibility too. This can never be a one-sided relationship. That is why the agreement in the beginning of this re-lationship is so important. Nobody stands irresponsible at any time in this relationship. Each party has a responsibility! The agreement is the foundation upon which this relationship is built. Unless there is a proper agreement, situations like these can be the reason why many athletes eventually give up, and why many coaching relationships in the past have turned sour!

Few coaches have an agreement. Most coaches have an assumption. Few coaches are willing to draw up a formal agreement in the begin-ning of a relationship regarding the responsibilities of each party. Few coaches know what they are willing to commit to and few coaches know what they expect from their athletes! Most of the time coaching relationships are built on common sense. Common sense is an idea, not a principle. Any relationship built on common sense will at some time lead to dreadful disappointment when we find that we all have different ideas about life. An agreement gives clarity. Common sense is vague.

THE "GUILT-GRIP" OF THE SCHOOL COACH.

A major reason for athlete burn-out, athletes who quit, physical inju-ries, etc. is the fight for fame amongst school coaches. At a young age we often find that naturally talented children rise head and shoulders above their peers. It is common to find naturally talented children who can do everything better than their peers at a very young age.

Every coach wants (his team) to be successful. The inclusion (and commitment) of these stars are essential, especially at school level. Every coach wants these children to prefer his particular sport / discipline. Every coach wants these children to be loyal to him. The battle to "own" these stars often becomes ridiculous and it comes at a big price: We lose the hearts and the joy of these natural stars. *Once a coach uses guilt as a motivational factor, he loses all authority and trust*. You never win an athlete's heart with guilt! You win an athlete's heart with honesty and integrity.

A real coach has an agreement with his athletes. If an athlete cannot abide by the initial agreement, he cannot be selected for the team. You never use emotional guilt to get an athlete to choose. Your acceptance of people and your relationship with them is built upon honesty and the initial agreement you make with them. If you make an agreement – stand by it! Never desist from your word (agreement)! Make sure that your agreement is clear as to what you expect of your athletes once they decide to make use of you as their coach.

Stories of athletes being disappointed by their coaches are numerous! Many of you reading this book can testify to the intense disappointment you had in coaches. Many talented athletes' reasons for quitting their sports and their dreams are locked up in their disappointments regarding their coaches. Are they correct in their judgements? Of course they are! Feelings are real. If the person working with you does not know how to deal with you in a correct manner, he is probably not qualified to work with you either.

The first qualification for teaching / leading / mentoring is to accept that someone else thinks and responds to things differently than you will. This skill is called wisdom – knowing what to do with whom and when to do it! This is why the career of a coach is often compared to a roller-coaster ride. Exciting, thrilling, up and down... The first person to be questioned, once an athlete or team does NOT perform, is the coach and rightfully so! This is why it is so important for any coach to become more than just a specialist. Real coaches constantly grow in wisdom. They can never "arrive" (estimate themselves as being too important)!

There are a vast number of coaches who can testify to the disappointments they have experienced with their athletes (and the athlete's parents). They have legitimate reasons why they could not successfully coach an athlete or a team. Sometimes you end up in a situation where the two parties (coach and athlete) are not compatible. This could probably have been determined **before** entering into this relationship. Excuses are useless! Nobody is interested in the reasons why someone did not make it to the top. Life looks for people who can give reasons why and how they made it to the top!

THE WISE SCHOOL COACH

Any school coach know this: There are certain "stars" in any school. Every discipline (sport) wants to use these stars! Which discipline / sport should this child select and commit to?

What do you do when you know that this special child's heart (focus) is not your discipline, but another? Only a fool will throw aside the services and talents of such an athlete. If you are offended by his / her first choice you are probably not good enough yourself! No coach has the luxury to take offence. Life is not about you! This child's life (and choices) is about his own future, not your coaching career. We all know how vulnerable children are.

If a child's focus is on another sport, use his talents when you need him and when he is available, *but never at the cost of an athlete who is 100% committed*. Wisdom is essential. Every coach needs to have guiding principles regarding his reasons for selecting athletes.

One of the most important determining factors of success in life is OPPORTUNITY. You can never rob one athlete of an opportunity simply because another athlete has more talent (yet his level of commitment questionable). *Commitment is the determining factor to open the door to opportunities*. I have seen too many athletes with amazing talent, passionate parents and great coaches, yet they are spoiled, arrogant and not committed. They know that they will be chosen because of their talent, yet it always ends in disaster. No matter how talented a person is – if there is no commitment, opportunities will be wasted - at the cost of the dreams of less talented, yet totally committed children. This is wrong!

Life is about choices and accepting the consequences for one's choices. This is why the agreement in the beginning of a coaching relationship is so essential! As coach (especially at school level) you have the *responsibility of being fair and just*. For every reward in life there is also a price to pay.

We cannot allow the talented to get the rewards without paying the price. Eventually talent is NOT ENOUGH! Talent becomes an equalizer. Then commitment and character becomes the determining factors for success. Should we give preference to the talented at an early age at the cost of the committed? Is it not foolish and short-sighted? If someone does not understand commitment and sacrifice even the most talented often quits. Rather give the opportunity to the committed athlete because *with hard work and commitment you will go much further than with talent!*

We all want to win, but to win at the cost of a life, of hopes, of dreams and relationships? How can a real coach justify this? Don't be short-sighted (by talent) that you lose out on those true heroes (less talented but more committed) who will be the stars of our future if they are granted a fair opportunity. More hearts are broken and more spirits are lost because of foolish coaches who will do anything to get the talented to play at the cost of the committed. They do this because they have a fool's goal: To win a single game.

The challenge is to become so good at coaching that you can take average talent with amazing commitment and mould it into super-stars! Everybody (even the most talented) has to admit that we need to choose those who are focussed and committed if we really want to be successful. Commitment and sacrifice is the price; opportunity is the reward. That's life! People will accept it. Rather be respected by people than liked by them. You will go much further in your coaching career.

We know about coaches experiencing disappointments with their athletes. The question is: **"How do you avoid these disappointments?"** Who is the responsible party? The responsible party is the leader of this relationship: **It is you, the coach**! You have to know what level of commitment you are willing to give. You also have to know what you will be expecting from your athletes. You have to acknowledge what you know and also what you don't know yet! You have to know how much time you have available for this relationship and also what your limitations are. You have to know exactly where you will be willing to go. If you expect more from your athletes than they are willing to give then you are not the right coach for them. If you expect less from your athletes than they are willing to give then you are not the right coach either. *This relationship can only work if both of you are in agreement with each other!* Both parties have to know and accept personal responsibility in this relationship!

In the beginning of a coaching relationship, coaches usually get 100% commitment from their athletes. Athletes have a deep desire to trust their coach! For this same reason a coach have tremendous power. If you abuse this power and become too familiar with your athletes (when you forget whom you are working with), it is easy to become arrogant in this relationship. When this happens you might miss the moment of trust 100%! You can lose the heart (trust) of your athlete in a heated or unguarded moment. Athletes want to be loyal, but the moment you lose your athlete's trust, you usually lose their hearts as well!

I have witnessed many coaches becoming arrogant and blasé because of their years of experience and a couple of success records. Some have been instrumental (in some way) in the careers of champions. This success causes them to become so important (in their own opinion) that they forget the true purpose of coaching. *Coaching is NOT about you!* Coaching is about assisting someone else to become the champion the world dreams and speaks about.

I have witnessed coaches treating athletes with so much disrespect and arrogance it was astounding. They viewed themselves as gods because of the power they knew they had. Power over the image, the emotions and the behaviour of the athletes they work with. Some coaches view this power as their victory in life. They keep their athletes doubting themselves, believing that without the coach they are nothing. What a sad picture! How sorrowful to watch people engage in such a level of arrogance and exploitation. It is sad to see that brief and momentary successes are really many people's ruin in life.

We all understand that athletes, who constantly have to perform under emotional and physical pressures, are much more sensitive for fragile moments. You don't have the luxury of not being in the moment. You have to be in the moment at all times! You have to be super sharp regarding the emotional levels of your athletes. In one unguarded moment of weakness you might lose your athletes' total trust and commitment. This is probably the biggest demand upon coaching – your constant awareness of your athlete's emotional needs.

Here are a couple of fragile moments which I have witnessed and experienced in my own life:

1. A player makes a critical error during a match and the coach loses it! He immediately withdraws the player from the field whilst visibly displaying his disgust and anger. When the player comes off the field the coach either ignores him or belittles him with sarcasm. You can be sure – this player's heart is lost!

Correct behaviour: When a player makes a critical error (especially when working with children who are not professionals yet) you have to cover that player with words like: *"Don't worry – many of us has made that mistake before. Try again and simply trust that you will get* *it right sometime!"* You have to protect this player against ridicule and sick jokes from team mates at all cost. Some players might be able to deal with it, but most can't.!

2. A player comes to you and asks a question like: *"Coach, do you think I should change the grip on my racquet?"* This might be a rather useless question (common sense). The truth is that this player was just looking for some way of getting your emotional attention. If you answer this question with annoyance in your voice like: *"Ai man, do I look like your caddy?"* you can be sure that you missed the moment totally. By missing it – you might also lose the heart of your player...

Correct behaviour: Make effort with every (even idiotic) moment your players seek your attention. Many athletes are extremely insecure and will often seek assurance in an immature way. Have enough wisdom *not to* expose them. Cover them and then coach them! Rather answer this question with something like: *"What do you think? Will it be better for you or not?"* Agree with their choice (there is really no right or wrong) and teach them to take personal responsibility in the future.

3. A player gives his best effort but still manages to make a huge mess. His team mates have a good laugh and the coach joins in. BIG mistake! Whenever someone gives his best effort you have to protect that person irrespective of the outcome of his effort. Many athletes lose their willingness to take risks (courage) because they fear the ridicule should they not succeed.

Correct behaviour: In that specific moment (not later), stop every activity and reward that player verbally for his effort and his guts. Tell everyone else that this attitude is exactly what you are looking for. You are looking for athletes who are willing to take risks. Protect the player and reward him in front of others!

4. An athlete loses a game / race he could and should have won. The worst thing you can do is to show your disappointment by avoiding or ignoring this athlete. Expressing your disappointment verbally or non-verbally in this moment can be fatal. These are moments in which athletes can be broken or where you can literally save them! Rejection is the worst thing you can do in a trusting relationship.

Correct behaviour: This is a moment in which your wisdom as coach is tested. Do you stand **with** your athlete in this moment of embarrassment and failure or do you disappear from the scene and leave your athlete alone to face the heat? Understand that success is a journey and not a result! Go to your athlete and say: *"I understand your disappointment and this excites me because now I know that your dream is important to you. Let's learn from today – it is a painful lesson but a necessary one. This happens to the best in the world! The aim is to learn from this and do it different next time... Let's move on."*

In competition at the highest level, talent, technique and physical ability are merely equalizers. The differentiator is the character and the heart of your athlete. If there is no heart, success is almost impossible. There comes a point where talent alone will not take you through. These are the moments created by amazing relationships and real coaches.

WINNING THE HEART OF YOUR ATHLETE

A heart is more easily won in an environment of safety. *It all starts with an agreement*. You stick to your agreement! You give direction and certainty *before* you enter into a coaching relationship. You stick to your word even though your athlete might fail you initially. You remain in control of your emotions. You remain in control of this relationship. You don't take things personally. Every athlete will fumble (lose their cool / make idiotic decisions / disappoint you) from time to time. When they let slip, they will obviously break this agreement. You might be disappointed, but remember – it is temporary. *You are busy with a process!* This is some of the worst challenges you will face in growing into a real coach. ***Personal disappointments***... You have to know how much you are willing to endure and where you draw the line. Drawing a line is only possible if there is an agreement! Without an agreement there is no accountability and many relationships have suffered severely because of this.

It almost sounds like being a real coach is more intense than a marriage or raising children!

Believe me – it is just as intense and it is even more emotional than a marriage. You commit yourself to become part of someone's dream in life! How much more personal can you get? This is not a relationship and commitment you mess with – it is serious stuff! Even on the lowest level. ***Coaches are of the most influential people on this planet!*** They influence the biggest stars of our generations. They influence their hopes, their passions, their decisions, their relationships and also their performances. You can never think you are not important. You are! You never know who you may be working with right now. You may believe it is simply a naughty little boy or a stunning little girl, but what you have in your hands could be the next world champion or the next world leader! The influence you have on this child's life might change the course of humanity.

The question to the answer is: "*Are you ready and prepared for this responsibility? Are you prepared to commit to such an intense relationship? Are you prepared to be loyal in the most intense situations of pressure or disappointments?*" Be very sure about your answer! If you are not sure – rather commit to be a specialist. Someone who will only take responsibility for coaching a technique and a skill, but that is it. ***Rather commit to less and give more instead of committing to become a real coach, when you are merely willing to function as a specialist***. Be big enough to commit to less in the beginning and eventually be able to give more, instead of committing to the whole package and ending up being unable to deliver.

As a matter of fact – that is probably where every coach should begin! Begin small and grow big instead of promising big and produce small.

First qualify yourself as a specialist in a certain area. Then go broader, give more than what is expected... Becoming a real coach is an amazing process... The more you engage, the more you will understand how uniquely special every human being is. The more you understand this, the more you will know that *intense personal involvement in the very core of someone's life is essential for growth – yet it needs to be done with true wisdom*!

In the beginning of this relationship you start off with building trust and loyalty. As soon as this trust has settled your athlete is going to allow you into his / her personal life (decision-makings, habits, friendships, choices, hopes and dreams). You will be able to expect almost anything from your athletes and they will be willing to do almost anything for you. Your athletes want to trust you with everything – the question is:

Are you trustworthy?

The moment you engage into a coaching relationship you give up many things. Things that are freely available to the average person. Things like emotional outbursts, verbal disappointments, anger, aggression, wild parties, getting intoxicated, being tired, no desire to give your best, loose morals, unacceptable behaviour, weak decisions, etc...

As a real coach you give up these luxuries. You commit to becoming a pillar of strength for someone else. You commit to becoming an emotional source of power. You become a mentor. As a mentor your task involves far more than simply teaching a skill. Teaching skills are based on theories and personal interpretations of other people's actions. Anyone can read a theory and proclaim to have the knowledge. There is a large number of books on a variety of techniques available in any bookstore. True, it is always valuable to read as much as possible because we can always gain more knowledge. Remember though that personal interpretation is unique. Just as unique as each athlete you work with. *Never try to duplicate*. *Try to embrace and nurture uniqueness*. Your own (in coaching) and your athlete's (in his / her technique). *Technique is an interpretation of a law – not a law in itself*.

> *Technique is an interpretation of a skill,*
> *not a law in itself!*

Every coach wants to believe that his / her interpretation of a technique is correct. It is correct - but there are other techniques that are also right. Different techniques are developed through different opinions and different interpretations, and they all have value. Unfortunately most people believe that if someone has a different interpretation / opinion, one party has to be wrong. ***Believing that is what's wrong***!

Thinking this way cause us to take offence and it gives us a critical eye (seeing mistakes) and not a possible-eye (seeing possibilities and solutions). Most coaches coach mistakes (they see mistakes and they constantly try to correct them). Almost anyone can see a mistake, but is that mistake truly a mistake or is it simply a technique that differs from your own interpretation of what's right? Believing that your interpretation of something is the only correct interpretation is wrong! World champions differ dramatically from each other regarding technique. Which one is then the correct one? True – there are basic principles underlying every successful technique, but eventually the successful technique is the technique that brings successful results!

To be successful in coaching there are a couple of critical elements. One of the most important elements is: ***Your athletes have to believe in themselves (not doubt themselves!)***. Once a technique is learnt, you have to go from learning to believing! Belief comes from repetition (conditioning) and success-experiences. You ingrain your athlete's unique technique by practicing the basics over and over. Eventually this effective technique will become an automatic action which can be performed in moments of being under intense pressure.

A big mistake made by many technical specialists (coaches) is the fact that they plant the seed of doubt in their athlete's minds. It does give a coach a measure of power if his athlete is dependent upon him. It is foolish to do so. Only a fool will believe that he can create a true champion by means of holding a winning card (measure of control) called doubt.

Faith is the foundation for performance. You have to believe that you can make it. You have to believe that what you do will work well enough! Even though your technique might look totally different from the next athlete's, it does not matter! Eventually it is all about your belief that you are capable of performing a task successfully in the moment of pressure with your own unique technique!

Technique is not about looks – it is all about basic principles applied correctly. This is why teaching young children the correct principles in the beginning of their sporting endeavours is so important! This is why the influence of a primary school coach is so dramatic! Their knowledge and understanding of the *basic principles* are essential. It can literally make or break an athlete's future!

How sad that we neglect the proper training and education of our primary school coaches. Once a child has learned the wrong principles (because of ignorance in coaching) the next coach will have to try and re-coach a technique whilst trying to keep the belief of the athlete as well. This is a huge challenge! Once you change a technique it almost always goes hand in hand with a drop in performance. Once performance drops, most athletes develop thoughts of doubt. *Doubt is any athlete's biggest enemy*!

Fortunately the human being is enormously adaptable and the process of changing a technique has been done with great success by thousands of athletes. We can successfully *un*-learn or reverse wrong principles (techniques) and learn the correct principles (new techniques). It does however take a very sensitive and competent coach to do this. The most important part of this process is to contain the belief and trust of your athlete whilst building your athlete's belief in his new technique.

For example: A youngster has been taught the wrong principles. Young children do things as they see them being done (monkey sees – monkey does)! Some children have a natural feel for a skill. Although they do it wrong, they might be successful at first. The primary reason for this initial success does not really lie in the technical skill level of the child – it is usually the level of incompetence of his peers and perhaps because of a quick growth curve in this particular child.

What it means is that some children stand out simply because of their physical size or because of a lack of ability in their opponents. Standing out means they get all the attention and once the system of performance-identification starts, they (or actually their parents) will soon be looking for a personal coach. Suggestions and questions will be asked *'whether we have a new champion in our family'*. This is the natural flow of life and this is how it should be! Success in life is largely dependent upon the opportunities one get. We are however, so often caught up in this race towards fame that we lose track of the process and are blinded by short-term results.

Natural talent could and should turn into a career opportunity. It is magnificent! This is the life many people dream of... to be able to do what you are naturally talented to do, to love what you do and then get paid for it! Parents aspire to give their children the best opportunities to live their dreams. The first step is getting a coach. They ask around. They hear about a specialist. This specialist immediately sees that the basics of the technique might not be correct. His first task is to start teaching the correct basics. Suddenly this child has to think about what he is doing and the freedom of movement disappears...

Movement become a conscious effort. This usually goes hand-in-hand with a drop in performance. When performance drops, so does the experience of success. Suddenly this child's motivation becomes a question. *Experiencing success is certainly the biggest source of motivation*. The personality of this athlete and the skills of this new coach (specialist) will determine whether this athlete will see it through or whether he / she will get stuck in a mud-pool of doubt and disappointment.

Many children become so negative and fearful of failure (especially if they were the champions since a young age) during this possible phase of changing a technique that some of the best just quit. They start to doubt themselves. In order to protect themselves emotionally they begin to predict and expect failure and mistakes. One would rather predict failure than hope for success and then not achieve it.

The ideal is that children will be taught the correct techniques (basic principles) in the beginning of their participation in sport!

The role of a coach is intense and extremely personal. A total coach is much more than just a specialist. There are many specialists but few "total coaches". The ideal is to become a ***total specialist coach***. Many coaches can coach a technique. Few coaches can coach an athlete. We find coaches who are amazing with people but sadly they know nothing about technique (the principles of movements). The goal is to master both: Coaching techniques and deal with people in wisdom! This will forever remain the challenge and the adventure of coaching...

4.

THE BEGINNING – THE AGREEMENT

A relationship can only work if the two (or more) parties involved stand in agreement as to where this relationship is going and what the role of each party is in this relationship. Without an agreement people work on assumptions. The results of assumptions are usually disappointment and regrets because we all assume differently...

How do you reach an agreement? It sounds so easy: *"Make an agreement"*. It is very much like the idea of setting goals. It sounds so easy to set goals. We read about the importance of setting goals and we hear successful people urging others to do it. How do you do it?

When you eventually take the time, sit down and start writing down your goals you will find that it is not so easy. As a matter of fact – most people NEVER get down to writing down their goals because they do not know what to write or how to write it! More than 95% of society will never get down and physically do what is essential to live a successful life. We all claim that we know what to do, yet who is doing it? Setting goals start with *seeing the end* and then writing them down.

Let's discuss an agreement. I will try to make it simple and give you an example of an agreement-conversation. In this example I refer to the male coach and a male athlete, but it really does not make a difference whether it is male or female. An agreement remains an agreement.

THE AGREEMENT-CONVERSATION: (THE PROCESS)

THE APPOINTMENT

Athlete's parents (to the new coach): *"Mr. X, we would like to find out whether you would be willing to coach our child. We have heard many positive things about you and would very much like you to impart your knowledge and wisdom in our child's life"*

Coach: *"Thank you for your trust in my – I value it highly. It will be a privilege to coach your child, but before we can engage on such a personal and important journey we will have to determine whether we will be able to walk this road together. We have to get to know each other and find out whether our expectations and aspirations are the same. I suggest we get together to discuss this.*

Parents: *"100%, coach. Can we arrange it for tomorrow morning at 10am?"*

Coach: *"Perfect, I will bring my thoughts. I would like you to bring your expectations and plans so that we can see whether this relationship can work."*

THE MEETING (WITH THE PARENTS)

If it is an individual sport – you make an appointment with the parents alone. If it is a team-sport it is imperative that the coach have a meeting with all the parents involved (as a group) **before** you have an agreement-conversation with the team.

Coach: *"It is great meeting you and thank you for your request. I would like to start this journey in the correct manner. It is imperative that we should agree upon your expectations from me, as well as* *my expectations from you (as parents as well as your child). If we agree, it will be a pleasure to work with your child."*

Parents: *"Thank you for your time and we believe that we will stand in agreement."*

Coach: *"Once you become involved in coaching someone you also become involved in a close personal relationship. As parents you are the most important people in your child's life and this is how it should be! If you grant me the freedom to speak into your child's life, we will have to stand in agreement because if we speak a different language it will never work.*

I have principles upon which I base my coaching. I also have certain expectations from my athletes. There are certain things I will request from you as parents, and you have to be comfortable with it. You also have to tell me what you expect from me. If we agree it will be a great privilege to support and guide your child towards achieving his dreams. If however you expect things from me of which I am not aware, and if I do things differently than you thought it would be done, we are setting ourselves up for disappointment. Your child will be the one suffering the consequences.

Does it all make sense to you?"

Parents: *"We agree 100%!"*

Coach: *"I am going to make an agreement with your child regarding a number of things. I would like to keep you in the picture:*

✓ *I commit to always be on time – If (due to unforeseen circumstances) I am not, I will let someone know and try to make sure that there is still proper leadership and guidance in the training session.*

✓ *I will expect the same from your child – to be on time all the time. If he cannot make it on time I will expect him to let me know within reasonable time.*

✓ *Before every training session I will explain what the goal and purpose of the session is – your child will therefore know what to expect.*

✓ *I will try in every way possible to act in a professional and ethical manner. I will deal with the personal issues of your child in this manner – I will keep it confidential except if I believe that the health of your child is threatened by keeping quiet.*

✓ *I will expect you and your child to "cover" me in my profession in the same way. If there is anything that upsets you or your child I would want you to discuss it with me and not spread rumours and stories. I know that I am not above making mistakes. I know that I am not perfect. I will always listen to suggestions and ideas but you have to understand that I cannot apply every idea or every technique in every book. I commit to constantly keep on top of new ideas etc.*

✓ *I will deal with any technical challenge your child may experience in a professional way. If I do not have an answer I will find one.*

✓ *If a change in technique is the only way moving forward you have to know that your child's performance will most probably first plunge – which might cause doubt and concern (in your child and in you). It is imperative that belief and hope is never lost during such a process. Your constant encouragement and edification during such a phase is essential. If your child doubts me (as a coach) we are wasting our time...*

✓ *When we start this journey your child have to know that in order to become the best he will have to beat the best. It is foolish to look for an easy and comfortable road to achieving his dream. Your child will have to consciously choose to master the challenges along the way. Only in mastering the most difficult obstacles will one eventually become a true master. I do understand that there are certain times when one is just not on top of things (a bad day). I will always have grace. If your child wants to train with me, choosing comfort and looking for the easy way out is not an option. If he dreams of being the best, there can be no excuses in this journey.*

✓ *I am going to ask you specifically to support him in an emotionally distant way during competitions. All athletes go through emotional growth-phases. Emotional weakness is a phase where responsibility for decisions and actions are placed upon the presence and the pressures coming from the parents (if it is allowed.) I would like your child to become emotionally self-reliant as soon as possible. Once he is emotionally self-sufficient you can definitely move closer. I trust you to understand this.*

✓ *It is important that you will freely communicate with me, should you feel there are certain things present in his life I should be aware of. I would appreciate it.*

✓ *After competition your first line of feedback (whether your son won or lost) should ALWAYS be positive (except however in the case where your child has broken our agreement, lost his cool and threw a tantrum)! Acceptance and encouragement on this road to his dream is essential even though defeat and poor performances will sometimes be at the order of the day. It takes wisdom to guide someone to the top. Parents can sometimes be one of the biggest stumbling blocks because of unguarded moments of disappointment!*

✓ *There are certain characteristics I am going to expect from your child. I want to discuss this with you first. If I expect this but you don't, we set ourselves up for emotional battles in times of pressure.*

1. **Respect** – *for me as coach, for you as parents, for opponents (even though they themselves might be rude), for all officials and for the rules of the game.*

2. **Discipline** – *Always on time, always in proper control of his emotions and 100% commitment to effort.*

3. ***Sportsmanship*** – *I expect mature and orderly conduct from all my athletes at all times towards competition, authority and rules. When they are out there they represent more than just themselves. They represent you and they represent me.*

4. ***Emotional control*** – *One of the conditions in coaching your child is that he will have to commit to become mentally tough. Being mentally tough means no tantrums, no ridicule, no complaining, and no excuses. Every athlete I coach has to commit to take full responsibility for results even though there are often things outside of our control. That is life and we have to learn to master those situations as well. Things like bad referees, intimidating spectators, opponents who cheat etc. are part of competing and needs to be mastered if we want to become the best.*

5. ***Intensity*** – *The success of every training session is determined by your child's attitude towards it. I will expect a great attitude and a great attitude means high intensity. If your child does not have a great attitude the session might become a taboo-session which simply means that your child will not be allowed to take further part in that particular session. I do not believe in punishing athletes by means of physical training. Athletes must love physical training and should never see it as a form of punishment. Being able to train is a privilege – never a punishment! I will always give a clear warning before discarding any athlete from a training session.*

✓ *I undertake to keep you in the loop as far as possible. I will communicate with you at least twice a year to discuss your child's progress and my experience with him. We have to get together to plan your child's future from time to time.*

✓ *If you have any other requests or requirements – please feel free to do so now.*

Parents: *"This is 100%, coach. We support you in all of this and we are excited about the journey ahead of us!"*

Coach: *"Thanks. I value your understanding and I will give my best to guide and coach your child to be able to live and achieve his dreams. Now we have to hear from him whether he buys into this team..."*

THE AGREEMENT (WITH THE ATHLETE/S)

Note:

i. This is the meeting between the coach and a team (rugby / netball / cricket / hockey etc.) in the beginning of a season.

ii. I refer to the singular athlete in my conversation, but it is also applicable for the plural (team).

Coach: *"Thanks for your time and for being on time. Before we start this journey and this season we have to agree upon what we all expect from each other. We have to know what our aim is and whether we will be a team. I know that you are striving to reach your dream and I do not take assisting you light-heartedly! I have already had a great conversation with your parents regarding their expectations from me and my expectations from this relationship. They are OK with it. You and I have to reach an agreement before we can continue.*

Firstly I would like to ask you: "What are your dreams / goals with this sport?"

Athlete: *"Wow coach, I would like to become a Springbok / I would like to become one of the best in the world (or if it is a team – we would like to win the cup)."*

Note: You will find that many children are afraid to dream really big. You have to stimulate and inspire them to dream big. A big dream will take a huge commitment whilst small dreams are easily discarded and left. They might need to hear your dream first (which will tell them where you are willing to go / dream).

> **Coach:** *"Great! I am so glad that your dream is really big and inspiring! How do you think you are going to accomplish this dream? Do you believe it is going to be a walk in the park (easy) or do you believe that you will sometimes have to do more than you think is possible? Do you believe that you will have to master the most difficult circumstances in order to become the best?"*
>
> **Athlete / team:** *"There are going to be hindrances for sure, coach – I do not believe it is going to be a walk in the park. I will have to work really hard."*
>
> **Coach:** *"Knowing this - would you like me to make me it easy and comfortable for you or would you like me to make it difficult and challenging for you?"*
>
> **Athlete / team:** *"The only way to reach my dream is to master the most difficult circumstances. I would like to ask you to make it tough for me, coach – please do not make it easy and comfortable."*
>
> **Coach:** *"Great! This is a wise decision. Well done! Of course we are going to have lots of fun and joy in this journey, but our aim is to become a master in all circumstances! What is your attitude going to be when we have high pressure training sessions? Are you going to moan and groan or are we going to work as a team?"*
>
> **Athlete / team:** *"We are going to be a team, coach and I will never moan and groan! I will tackle every challenge with a great attitude!"*
>
> **Coach:** *"I had a feeling you would say that... Is this an agreement? Are you telling me that I will never have to convince you to train hard? Are you telling me that you will never moan and groan with a negative attitude?"*
>
> **Athlete / team:** *"It's a deal coach! I commit to it!"*

Coach: *"Fantastic – I really look forward to working with you! Next point. I would like to honour our relationship. One way is to honour your time. I commit to always be on time and if I cannot be, I will let you know. Can I expect the same from you? If for some reason you cannot make it on time will you let me know? If I cannot make it to a training session I will definitely let you know and I will either arrange for someone to stand in for me or I will give you the exercises for the day which you will then do on your own. I do however not plan for this to happen. Is this OK with you?"*

Athlete / team: *"It is 100%, coach"*

Coach: *"Thanks for that. Our next subject is self-motivation and self-discipline. I am a coach who works with people who wants to work and become better. My work is to motivate, not to criticize. Is this OK with you? Are you prepared to take responsibility? I am there to assist you and support you in reaching your dream – I will not force you to live your dream! For that reason I will ask you to take charge of a training session from time to time. I would like to see what you are willing to do on your own – without me spurring you on. Will that be OK with you?"*

Athlete / team: *"Yes coach – it is 100%. I would love to do it!"*

Coach: *"Awesome! The next point is quite personal. I know that all of us go through situations in life that might be challenging. Everything influences us in some way. I want to ask you to be open and frank with me regarding personal issues. If I don't know what you are going through I might not understand you correctly and it may cause a misunderstanding.*

Know this – I will never feel sorry for you because I know that every challenge is an opportunity for another victory. Challenges will come your way and they need to! I will simply better understand you by sharing what's happening in your life. You will rid yourself from excuses and feeling sorry for yourself. There is an answer to every challenge – I will find it with you!

Athlete / team: *"100%, coach!"*

Coach: *"Great – I will always back you but you have to back me. Are you willing to be open and truthful towards me?"*

I have to make certain decisions. Am I always 100% sure and 100% correct? Impossible! We are living an adventure and I will at all times give it my best effort to make the best possible decisions for you. Truths differ. You might sometimes feel that you do not agree with the decisions I make. It is in those moments that the strength of our relationship will be tested! **You have to trust me even if I think differently from you.** *You can always question me, but you have to respect and commit to my decisions, otherwise this relationship will never work! If I ask you to walk on your hands you will have to believe that there is a plan and reason behind it. Your belief in what I tell you to do is not about whether I am right – it is all about the belief you have in our team!*

When I made a mistake I will acknowledge it and ask your exoneration. It is impossible to go through this adventure without taking risks. Risks mean that we might sometimes fail! The bottom-line is – we have to remain a team!

Athlete / team: *"This is 100%, coach."*

Coach: *"There are a couple of things I have already discussed with your parents. I need to get your buy-in and commitment regarding this as well:"*

✓ *Before every training session I will tell you what we are going to do and what the purpose of it is. You will know what to expect from every training session.*

✓ *I will, at all times, try to conduct myself in a professional manner. It means that I will regard our relationship as professional. I will respect your privacy and your confidentiality. I will however not remain quiet if I believe that my silence will not be to your benefit. I will at all times be 100% discreet.*

✓ *I expect that both you and your parents will protect and cover my professional image. If there is something you do not agree with, I expect you to discuss it with me personally and not spread rumours or gossip. I am only human and I may sometimes be wrong. I commit to stay on top of all new techniques and developments in order to assist you best.*

✓ *If you ever experience difficulty with certain techniques we will address it immediately with the best advice. If I cannot assist you, we will get help!*

✓ *When your technique needs to be adapted, you have to remember that your performance level will probably plunge at first before it will improve. You have to commit to stay in the process and never quit on yourself or on me. This is how thousands of athletes have succeeded on the road to success. As your body develops and grows your technique might need slight alterations. We have to find what works best for you in that particular stage of your development. Do you understand this process and are you committed to see this through?*

✓ *I understand that everyone occasionally has a difficult day. I am not blind to emotional needs. However, we don't have the luxury to indulge in emotional outbursts or tantrums. We are a team and we respect each other irrespective of how we feel. Is that OK with you?*

Note: In the case of working with female athletes it is imperative that the coaches are familiar and aware of athletes' menstrual cycles. Female athletes are often far more dependent upon emotional strength and support from coaches than male athletes.

✓ *My goal is to equip you best to achieve your dreams and goals. If you are here simply to have a good time you better tell me because I need to know what to expect from you. If you are here to become the best, the intensity and demands of training will be totally different. It takes more discipline and more effort if you want to become more than average.*

✓ *I have asked your parents not to attend your training sessions. If you are constantly aware of your mom or dad's approval or disapproval of what we are doing, it will never work. On the other hand – when you make mistakes (which you definitely will) I do not want you to be worried about what your mom or dad will think sitting next to the field. I want you to be free to try different things. I want you to make mistakes and learn from them. If you fear failure you will never make it. You have to be willing to take risks and enjoy the adventure thereof.*

✓ *I have also spoken to your parents regarding their behaviour at competitions. I want them to be there, but at a distance. I don't want you to try and please them constantly. They can do nothing for you during competition – you have to find your own way to deal with things.*

✓ *There are certain characteristics I will expect from you. If we do not agree on this then I am not the right coach for you:*

1. **Respect** - *for me as coach, for your parents, for officials (although they might sometimes be wrong) for your opponents and for the rules of the game.*

2. **Discipline** – *I will expect you to be on time for our appointments and practices, to be in control of your emotions at all times (you never have the luxury to throw your toys), to be committed in our sessions and to stick to our agreements.*

3. **Sportsmanship** – *I expect mature and proud conduct in all forms of competition, authority and rules.*

4. **Emotional control** – *This is one of the conditions for me coaching you. You have to commit to become mentally tough. Mental toughness means no arrogance, no tantrums, no complaints and no excuses. You will at all times have total responsibility for your conduct and for the results you deliver. I know unforeseen and*

uncontrollable events will happen. All this influences results in various ways – you have to deal with it. That is what it takes to get to the top. Overcoming the negatives such as unfair referees, extreme weather, opponents cheating, rude supporters, etc. are part of what it takes to eventually become a true master.

5. *Intensity – The success of every training session is 100% dependent upon your attitude. I commit to give it my best at all times. I will expect the same from you. There will be times to relax and have fun and then we will do so. If you are negative and want to hold back on your efforts you have to tell me before a session. Breaking this agreement will result in a warning. Thereafter you will have a taboo session which simply means that you will be asked to leave and not participate in any further training. This is your dream and I never want to be responsible to convince you to live it!*

✓ *I plan to have a conversation with your parents at least twice a year to discuss your progress and the way forward.*

Is all of this OK with you?"

Athlete / team: *"It is perfect coach – I'm in!"*

Coach: *"Thanks – now we stand in agreement and we know what to expect from each other. Is there anything you would like to ask me at this moment?"*

Athlete / team: *"..................."*

Coach: *"Now we can officially start our new season. Thanks for your attitude – I look forward to walk this road with you. I will see you on Monday at 4pm."*

The appropriate thing to do at this moment is to greet each athlete with a hand-shake. This serves as a bond and confirms your agreement. When you work with young girls a handshake might be a bit too formal. Start with a handshake but then (as you are lead by trust and common sense) you move towards a shoulder hug. Important – always keep it professionally-personal. Avoid kissing on the mouth (a cheek-kiss might be appropriate from time to time). Kissing on the mouth is too personal and might put you in an awkward position should your athlete numbers grow. Be consistent in how you deal with ALL athletes! *Greeting is essential and should be personal* – it confirms the trust and agreement between you and your athlete.

Personal accountability is now at the order of the day. The agreement is the guideline for responsibilities and the relationship.

This agreement-conversation sounds simple and easy and it is...! It is just as easy (and more comfortable) NOT to do! Be honest: How many of you have had such a conversation with one of your coaches during your life-time? Not many!

> *There is an extremely powerful thought*
> *about success in life:*
> *A thing easy to do is also a thing easy not to do.*
> *The difference between success and failure*
> *are usually easy things...*

WHILST TALKING ABOUT EASY THINGS HERE ARE A FEW TO CONSIDER:

? Is it easy to have an agreement-conversation with your athletes?

? Is it easy to write out your program / exercise plans for the afternoon and have them prepared before your training session?

? Is it easy to get a verbal commitment from your athletes before the start of every training session?

? Is it easy to keep to your rules? If not – consider a different career.

? Are these things a habit in your life or is today a good time to start?

Success is available to everyone who is willing to do the easy things. Failure on the other side is usually the result of neglecting or forsaking the easy things... Many coaches base their coaching on assumptions (how it should be). Assumption is the recipe for disappointment, regrets and broken relationships. Many stories of regrets and disappointments in people are the result of assumptions...

It is a known fact that the most important part of any project is how it begins. The most important part of any building is its foundation (the beginning). The most important part of life is our youth (the beginning) where our personality, our beliefs and our values are formed. The most important part of coaching is the agreement (when the relationship starts / at the beginning of a new season). A proper agreement will set the table for a fine dish! Enjoy it!

5.
SETTING GOALS AT THE BEGINNING OF A NEW SEASON

HOW DO YOU DO IT?

Steven Covey in his famous book: "Seven habits of highly successful people" makes a statement where he suggests: *Successful people begin with the end in mind*. Throughout life this is an extremely valuable principle – without knowing where you are going you will live a busy, yet insignificant life because you will be without direction. You will wake up and react to what life brings your way every day. The sad thing is that the majority of society live like this – extremely busy but going nowhere!

Most of you reading this are probably familiar with the importance of proper goal-setting. Not only regarding finances but also regarding your physique, your family, your marriage, your occupation, your health, etc. Research has found that proper goal-setting have a dramatically positive effect on any aspect of life once you do it properly! Most people know this. It is not new, yet if I ask you: *"Can you take me home and show me where you have written down your goals for this year and for the next five years regarding every aspect that is important to you? (Family / health / finances / sport / spirituality / mental health / etc...)"*. Can you take me home and show me? Few of you will be able to do it.

Your answer will be the same as the majority of people: *"I know what I want and where I am going but I have not written it down yet."* I can only smile. You might know about the importance of setting goals, but you have no understanding of the power thereof! You have not done it. It is therefore impossible to experience the benefits thereof!

We know many things, but we don't fully understand all of it. True understanding only takes place when you have to put your knowledge into action, or if you have to explain it to someone. Understanding is a much higher level of functioning than having knowledge. Knowledge is available to everyone (in heaps)! Surfing the internet will put you in contact with more knowledge you will be able to digest in a life-time. Knowledge not transferred into understanding means little.

How do you teach something if you do not understand it yourself? How can a coach teach a technique to an athlete if he does not understand the key-elements and the key principles underlying the successful execution of the technique? *Many coaches try to coach or change a technique as he has seen / read it in a book. The key principles in applying the technique is however a mystery because the coach doesn't understand them (has never experienced or performed them himself)*!

Technique is very specific and unique to each individual. We all differ in our basic DNA (our muscle strength, muscle type, length, weight, centre of gravity, bone density, endurance, way of thinking etc.). There are basic principles underlying every technique but the execution thereof might and probably will differ significantly from athlete to athlete. Trying to look like someone else is one of the biggest mistakes many coaches and many athletes make! It is not about looking (appearance?). It is about finding what works for you!

Doubt is any sportsman's biggest enemy. If you doubt your technique you are doomed to failure. When the pressure is rising, so will your doubt increase. When you doubt you will never follow through. You won't commit and success will be pure luck.

Setting goals in the beginning of a season / career is essential. This is the second step after finalizing the agreement. Every athlete (and every coach) needs to know exactly where they are going or what they are aiming for. Clear goals give direction and enable us to evaluate our progress which serves as a source of motivation.

Many athletes and coaches make the mistake of setting outcome goals instead of process goals.

What are outcome goals?

→ "I want to win a match"
→ "I want to make the team"
→ "We want to win the competition"
→ "I want to become number one"
→ "I want to become a Springbok"

When you look at these goals you will agree that most of them are written on the draw-board of many coaches and athletes. They are actually not goals – they are dreams! There is a major difference between a dream and a goal. **A dream is an achievement – an end-result. A goal is the steps that will take you to your dream**.

Many people's lives are a desperate struggle for survival. Not because they don't have dreams but because they never sat down to plan how to achieve them. What goals do you need to master in order to live your dreams? Most people never take the first step towards their dreams because they don't have a first step. They don't know how to set goals. People don't set goals because they are afraid to look foolish.

> *A dream is an achievement - an end-result.*
> *A goal is the steps that will take you to your dream.*
> *A great goal is never a result. It is a simple step!*

A great goal is never a result! Results are unknown and out of our control. How can we control the performance of another? The uncertainness of results is what gives sport and competition its colour. The uncertainness is part of the romance of competition. Uncertainty about the result produces the adrenalin for competition. Pressure is the sweet juice of life. It causes our blood to pump with passion and vigour. Too few are lucky enough to taste life. Too many are living in comfort. Too few know the feeling of passionate and vigorous living. Too many are just making a living. Society conditions us to look for the easy, the comfortable and the safe but in comfort and in safety there is no adrenalin, no hope and no need for a leap of faith.

We all dream about positive results, yet if victory is certain, competition will lose its attraction. Effective goals are those little steps we need to take in order to move closer to achieving our dreams. Big dreams are essential! We need to dream about stuff that takes our breath away. We need to dream about stuff that keeps us lying awake at night... We need to dream about things that are bigger than us!

A wise coach understands that reaching goals starts with small baby steps. We all learned to walk. We all realise that the first steps are always uncertain and wobbly. It takes **time** and **repetition** to become certain. Eventually we all walk with confidence. Once walking is mastered we move to jogging and then running. We will (all of us) often fall in this process of improving our ability to move. Sometimes we grow so confident that we forget to look out for the simplest obstacles. We might fall over the smallest stone. We call this experience. This process never ends! We constantly grow in **wisdom and experience.** Some of us gain more experience than others because some of us ask more and better questions. Eventually our mistakes become less and we are able to **take more risks.** We begin to understand our abilities. This is a never-ending adventure because even the most experienced people still fumble from time to time...

Success and life is a process. You can never run before you mastered walking. You can't take big risks without knowledge and experience regarding your abilities and skills. Abilities and skills are increased as we spend time practising and repeating the movements. We can never neglect the simple small steps because they will forever be part of the process of improvement! Mistakes will always be part of this process. It is the only way in which we grow our understanding of laws and principles of the skills we hope to master. The aim is to limit the mistakes and increase the experience of success.

HOW AND WHAT TYPE OF GOALS SHOULD YOU SET?

HERE ARE A FEW POINTERS TO TAKE NOTE OF:

→ Everything starts with a dream. Dream BIG!

→ You cannot give your dream to your athletes. You have to find your athlete's dream and use that as your compass in working with him!

→ Once you know your athlete's dream, you ask: *"How do you think we are going to get there?"*

→ Your athlete will answer something like: *"I will have to work hard and be prepared to put in extra time."*

This is the moment you move towards setting proper goals!

> *Successful people begin with the end in mind.*
>
> - Steven Covey -

THE CONVERSATION

Coach: *"You are correct in saying that you will have to work hard, but this is too vague. We have to be clear as to what we need to do in order to reach your dream. We need to be able to measure your progress. You need to be in control of your progress. We cannot measure your growth in results – it will be foolish! Let's rather identify the skills you need to master in order to move towards your dream. Let's write them down."*

Put a pen and paper in front of your athlete and tell him to write down the things you discuss. **Give control of writing this down to the athlete – don't do it yourself!**

Every sport has certain *key skills* which need to be mastered in order to become a true master. There are also essential *invisible skills* which eventually distinguish the best from the rest. It is imperative that your knowledge about both these skills is as wide as possible. You have to be thoroughly aware of all them in order to properly assist your athlete in setting goals. If you personally did not take part at a top-level you have to find someone who did. Ask that person about his experience. Ask him about the key skills as well as the invisible skills. If you have only taken part in a sport at school level it doesn't mean that you know and understand the skills and demands necessary to make it. First learn before you try to teach! Once you know the demands and the key factors, discuss them with your athlete.

For the purpose of this book I use tennis as example to illustrate such a goal-setting conversation:

Coach: "What do you believe are the necessary skills you need to master in tennis?"

Athlete: *"All the different shots, coach. A fore-hand, a back-hand, a serve, a volley, a smash, a drop-shot..."*

Coach: *"You are 100% correct. This is where we will begin. Is there anything besides hitting shots you need to master?"*

Athlete: *"I will have to work hard coach and I will have to be fit. I will need to improve in my ability to play."*

Coach: *"You are right again. Fitness is essential, but so is power, flexibility and speed. Besides this, do you think there is anything else?"*

Athlete: *"Wow coach, I am not sure? Is there?"*

Coach: *"You need to know – to become the best (to reach your dream) you have to master **every little thing there is to master!** I have made a list. Listen and if you want to, add anything!"*

THE LIST

- ✓ Firstly, there are the various **shots in tennis** – forehand, backhand, serve, volley, drop-shot, lob, smash, etc.

- ✓ Then there are **many variations on each shot**. There is a topspin and a cut, an attacking shot and a defensive shot. There is a drop-shot and a lob, etc.

- ✓ There are **different situations** you will need to master. For example, what to do when the momentum is on your side or what to do when the momentum is with the opponent.

- ✓ There are certain **critical moments** in a match – you need to learn to master such moments.

- ✓ There are **moments of pressure** – spectators next to the court, family of your opponents, challenging weather conditions, fatigue, referees, tight matches, finals.

- ✓ You need to learn to play **different strategies** – you have to master playing every opponent in the correct way.

✓ You need to learn **how to win**.

✓ You have to learn **how to bounce back after defeats,** *keeping your hopes, your dreams and your belief alive.*

✓ You need to learn to **mature in your ability to deal with both success and failure.**

✓ You have to learn **how to deal with pressure once you become the one everyone else wants to win**.

✓ You need to learn **how to fight from behind** – to **never say die, even if you face match-point against you!**

✓ You have to learn **how to maintain an attacking attitude** *even though you might be ahead!* **You can never win if you start to defend**.

✓ You need to learn **never to compare yourself to others,** *but to* **set your own standards in life and in your tennis.**

✓ You have to learn to **act with wisdom** *– you cannot take everything that comes your way personal. You need to be* **mentally tough!**

✓ You have to be **able to deal with arrogant and negative opponents without becoming arrogant yourself.**

✓ You have to **remain humble in your victories** *and value the small things in life.*

✓ You have to be a **worthy hero,** *an inspiration to others.*

✓ You do **not have the luxury of being average** *if you choose to be a champion.*

✓ You need to **choose your friends wisely** *because the wrong friends have been the down-fall of many potential champions!*

✓ You have to **master time,** *for time never stops running. If you waste it your dreams will run through your fingers like time runs out.*

✓ You need to be **focussed, able to withstand the attractions (distractions)** of lust, pleasure, fame, wealth and short-term pleasure.

✓ You have to **remain rooted in your values and morals** for fame has a strange way of sweeping the best off their feet.

✓ You need to be **fitter, faster, stronger and more flexible than others.**

✓ You need to learn to **eat correctly, to live a disciplined life and to make wise decisions.** One wrong decision might mean the end of your dream!

✓ You will have to learn **how to communicate with the press and with the public. You need to master public speaking.**

✓ You have to **remain positive in disappointing moments.**

✓ You need to **control your emotions in all circumstances.**

✓ You need to **be teachable at all times,** but to apply wisdom in being coached. You cannot take everything said by others on board. You need to **pick the people you allow to speak into your life with wisdom** – not with comfort!

✓ You have to **go the extra mile, to endure more, to suffer more and to be more persistent and patient than anybody else.**

✓ You need to **keep on believing** for without faith, life is hopeless and meaningless.

Are you ready for all this?"

Athlete: "Wow coach, I never thought about all these things... Yes, I want to go all the way!"

Coach: "Great! Let's come to an agreement. You are going to master all these things. **Therefore you have to agree and commit NOT to measure your success in terms of the results of your matches in the short term!** Winning matches will take care of itself the moment *you are ready for it. If your opponent is still better than you – you win the experience and he wins the match. It cannot delay your progress or take your focus away from your dream!* **It is part of the process.** *There is no such thing as losing because you are a winner! You will believe like one, act like one and become one. The results of a match will not change it. Losing is a mindset – but so is winning.* **From now on you think like a winner!** *If someone asks you about a match, your answer is always the same. You say: "I won and I am excited about it." If you don't win a match, you win experience, but you always win! Is it clear?*

Athlete: *"Yes coach – it is clear. It sounds awesome... always winning!"*

Coach: *"Remember – what you think about is where you are going. If you think about mastering small steps (making your goals) your body prepare for it and you will do it. Focussing your energy on winning is rather fickle – winning is a result (as is losing), but the uncertainty of winning naturally gets your body to fear losing.*

Losers fear losing. Winners focus on mastering small steps and they always win -either the match or experience! We will have a goal for every training session. We have to be 100% satisfied in mastering every possible step reaching your dream. Are you ready for it?"

Athlete: *"I am ready, coach!"*

Coach: *"I want you to go home and write down every small step (goal) you can think of. We will tick them off one by one."*

Athlete: *"Great, I will do so coach!"*

It is imperative that the athlete has to spend time thinking of all the possible goals he needs to master in order to achieve his dream. Athletes will often identify things they might see as personal challenges – you want to know about it! Therefore the athlete has to do this exercise on his own. Each of us sees challenges differently.

An example of such a goal chart

Goal chart (tennis)

Skill / attribute	Level of mastering
Forehand (topspin)	1 2 3 4 5 6 7 8 9 10
Forehand (slice)	1 2 3 4 5 6 7 8 9 10
Forehand (crosscourt)	1 2 3 4 5 6 7 8 9 10
Forehand (down the line)	1 2 3 4 5 6 7 8 9 10
Forehand (inside out)	1 2 3 4 5 6 7 8 9 10
Forehand (middlecourt)	1 2 3 4 5 6 7 8 9 10
Forehand (approach)	1 2 3 4 5 6 7 8 9 10
Forehand (halfcourtvolley)	1 2 3 4 5 6 7 8 9 10
Forehand (volley – above the shoulder)	1 2 3 4 5 6 7 8 9 10
Forehand (volley – lower down)	1 2 3 4 5 6 7 8 9 10
Forehand (dropshot)	1 2 3 4 5 6 7 8 9 10
Forehand (drive-volley)	1 2 3 4 5 6 7 8 9 10
Forehand (smash)	1 2 3 4 5 6 7 8 9 10
Forehand (smash behind)	1 2 3 4 5 6 7 8 9 10
Forehand (lob)	1 2 3 4 5 6 7 8 9 10
Forehand (recovery after lob)	1 2 3 4 5 6 7 8 9 10
Backhand (topspin)	1 2 3 4 5 6 7 8 9 10
Backhand (slice)	1 2 3 4 5 6 7 8 9 10
Backhand (crosscourt)	1 2 3 4 5 6 7 8 9 10
Backhand (down the line)	1 2 3 4 5 6 7 8 9 10

Backhand (middle court)	1 2 3 4 5 6 7 8 9 10
Backhand (approach)	1 2 3 4 5 6 7 8 9 10
Backhand (halfcourtvolley)	1 2 3 4 5 6 7 8 9 10
Backhand (volley – above the shoulder)	1 2 3 4 5 6 7 8 9 10
Backhand (volley – lower down)	1 2 3 4 5 6 7 8 9 10
Backhand (dropshot)	1 2 3 4 5 6 7 8 9 10
Backhand (drive-volley)	1 2 3 4 5 6 7 8 9 10
Backhand (smash)	1 2 3 4 5 6 7 8 9 10
Backhand (smash behind the head)	1 2 3 4 5 6 7 8 9 10
Backhand (lob)	1 2 3 4 5 6 7 8 9 10
Backhand (recovery after being lobbed)	1 2 3 4 5 6 7 8 9 10

Serve

Flat serve	1 2 3 4 5 6 7 8 9 10
Topspin-serve	1 2 3 4 5 6 7 8 9 10
Slice-serve	1 2 3 4 5 6 7 8 9 10

Mental toughness

Attack whilst under pressure	1 2 3 4 5 6 7 8 9 10
Dealing with negative opponents	1 2 3 4 5 6 7 8 9 10
Come-back from behind	1 2 3 4 5 6 7 8 9 10
Be in front and win	1 2 3 4 5 6 7 8 9 10
Change of strategy when an opponent "zone"	1 2 3 4 5 6 7 8 9 10
Patience in all circumstances	1 2 3 4 5 6 7 8 9 10
Wise decisions under pressure	1 2 3 4 5 6 7 8 9 10
Remain calm and positive in ALL circumstances	1 2 3 4 5 6 7 8 9 10
Always in control of emotions	1 2 3 4 5 6 7 8 9 10
Set the standard and don't conform to average	1 2 3 4 5 6 7 8 9 10

High intensity during training sessions	1 2 3 4 5 6 7 8 9 10
High intensity during matches – focus!	1 2 3 4 5 6 7 8 9 10
Play critical points with wisdom	1 2 3 4 5 6 7 8 9 10
Ability to swing momentum	1 2 3 4 5 6 7 8 9 10
Ability to keep momentum	1 2 3 4 5 6 7 8 9 10
Teachable Receptive? and not have an answer ready	1 2 3 4 5 6 7 8 9 10
Take responsibility and never have an excuse!	1 2 3 4 5 6 7 8 9 10
Recovery of injuries	1 2 3 4 5 6 7 8 9 10

Fitness and power

Endurance (5 km tot 10 km)	
Muscle-endurance (10 X 400 meter)	
Speed-endurance (10 X 100 meter)	
Power-endurance (3 sets) 20 x push-ups 40 x sit-ups push-ups 6 x pullups 20 x frog jumps 20 x Medicine ball shoulder throws 10 x Burpees	
Core-power –	
Flexibility Hamstring Hips Back Shoulders	

Public and human skills

Self-image (confession-talk)	1 2 3 4 5 6 7 8 9 10
Manners and appearance on the court	1 2 3 4 5 6 7 8 9 10
Communication skills (individuals)	1 2 3 4 5 6 7 8 9 10

Communication skills (groups)	1 2 3 4 5 6 7 8 9 10
Communication skills (opponents)	1 2 3 4 5 6 7 8 9 10
Communication skills (referees / officials)	1 2 3 4 5 6 7 8 9 10
Dealing with stressful events	1 2 3 4 5 6 7 8 9 10
Dealing with difficulties (family / friends)	1 2 3 4 5 6 7 8 9 10
Ability to learn from coach / parents / teachers	1 2 3 4 5 6 7 8 9 10
Dealing with success	1 2 3 4 5 6 7 8 9 10
Dealing with failure	1 2 3 4 5 6 7 8 9 10
Responses after victory	1 2 3 4 5 6 7 8 9 10
Responses after failure / defeat	1 2 3 4 5 6 7 8 9 10
Habits I would like to acquire:	
Time management (being on time and managing it)	1 2 3 4 5 6 7 8 9 10
Thoroughness – doing more than people expect	1 2 3 4 5 6 7 8 9 10
Promptness – doing things NOW not later!	1 2 3 4 5 6 7 8 9 10
Respect – humility and thankfulness	1 2 3 4 5 6 7 8 9 10
Excellence – proud of my decisions	1 2 3 4 5 6 7 8 9 10
"Dare" – willingness to take risks	1 2 3 4 5 6 7 8 9 10
Patience – to wait for the right moment	1 2 3 4 5 6 7 8 9 10
Emotional control – never take offence!	1 2 3 4 5 6 7 8 9 10
Neatness – always proud of how I look and my equipment. Always proud of my appearance and my equipment	1 2 3 4 5 6 7 8 9 10
Positive – always an optimist!	1 2 3 4 5 6 7 8 9 10
Faith – unwavering faith that everything is well	1 2 3 4 5 6 7 8 9 10
Generous – in giving without holding back	1 2 3 4 5 6 7 8 9 10
Comfortable – in all circumstances (no "issues")	1 2 3 4 5 6 7 8 9 10

Start to work on specific tasks. Determine which ones should be first. Decide how you will evaluate your level of mastering. Set a target date for each goal if possible.

Before every training session you and your athlete have to be clear about the goal(s) and purpose of the training session. After every session you should rate and evaluate the success of the training session. Training sessions will often have more than only one goal and purpose. Always incorporate those invisible skills which have much more to do with the emotional state of your athlete. Athletes should constantly be aware of the invisible skills.

The major purpose and function of proper goal-setting is motivation. *The strongest source of intrinsic motivation is the experience of success*. If you measure success according to results you are a fool. Your athletes will be up one day and down the next. Your work will become draining (convincing your athlete not to give up) instead of inspiring (enjoying mastering small steps). It is an energy-draining experience and a dreadful way of coaching.

When your aim is to master skills the probability of success is much higher than when your aim is winning. Winning is the result of mastering skills. Winning is a process – not really a result. Results are part of the process, but not the process as a whole. The process is infinitely bigger than results. A big mistake many coaches make is to step into the trap of measuring success by results. A true coach will imprint this on his athlete's minds: *Success is a mindset – not a result*! Winning a match is the result of mastering skills. Winning is fickle, uncertain and not supposed to be in your control – otherwise competition is useless. Winning is the product of doing the small things right.

Make sure that your athletes experience some form of success every day in every training session! Set proper goals before every training. If you don't, you waste opportunity and you miss out on intrinsic motivation which is readily available. Be wise – set goals and start living the dream.

6.
HOW DO YOU COACH SKILLS?

WHAT IS THE KEY TO SUCCESSFULLY TEACHING A SKILL?

Correct pictures! The human brain works in pictures. The moment we receive a message / command our brain goes to work to find relevant information that was stored in our brain (due to past experiences) to verify, compare or prepare us for an action. This picture from our past will immediately activate the relevant neural-pathways to cause the body (the muscles) to prepare for movement or action. If you don't have a reference for a certain action needed at a moment, it is very improbable that the action you perform will be correct. It will be an uneducated guess. We often see this when someone tries to perform an action which he has never done before. Usually it is rather funny.

If you want to witness the power of pictures look at your own mannerisms. Your way of talking, walking, doing, acting, etc. I will most probably see some of your parents' mannerisms in you. Children (if they are privileged enough to be growing up with their parents) often duplicate their parents' personal habits (i.e. talking, walking, eating, living, etc.). There is a well-known statement which is also the first key to coaching skills:

> *Monkey see... Monkey do...*

If you are a clever coach you will develop the technique of teaching skills by telling stories. Stories create pictures and pictures stick! Any athlete (young or old) will remember a story far better than a technical description of a technique. If you want your athlete to remain low, don't tell him to bend down – tell him to "duck the mud" (as if playing in a clay-fight)! It is fun, it is vivid and they remember stories!

THE BEGINNER:

Step 1: Before you explain the detail of a skill, take your athlete to a screen (television or computer), show a video of the skill you want to coach and allow your athlete to see how a master performs this skill in real life. Do this more than once – do it a couple of times! Say nothing – just let your athlete watch!

Step 2: Show the action again and use the slow-motion button. Talk your athlete through the action. Stop and pause. Explain key elements (moments) of the skill. These are things like balance, point of gravity, contact-point, position of the eyes, position of the feet, etc. Only identify crucial key elements at this moment (not all the fine detail). Keep it simple and easy. *Remember – it is far better to connect these principles to funny pictures or stories (ducking clay) than to explain it as it is*!

Step 3: Ask your athlete to explain what he has seen and heard. When your athlete explains the principles correctly, agree and reward him verbally. It builds confidence.

Step 4: Go to the court or field and start from the beginning. Move through the action step by step and allow your athlete to feel the movement. As you familiarise your athlete with each step, start combining the steps progressively. **Repetition is the key**! Repeat the correct movements until it becomes a natural movement. Remember to keep it simple. Too much technique and too much thinking will hinder progression. Progression is the key to motivation!

> "Repetition is the mother of learning,
> the father of action, which makes it the
> architect of accomplishment."
>
> - Zig Ziglar

THE AVERAGE TO TOP-ATHLETE:

The basics have been learned and technique is automated to a large extent. Repetition remains one of the most important principles to embed a skill in your neurological system. Getting something right once doesn't mean you have mastered it. It only means that your body has activated the correct neural pathway to execute the skill correctly. You have to stimulate that pathway again... and again... and again. Not by luck but by choice. The more you're able to find it the more you'll be able to control it. Once you can control it you can move to the next level of competing... **taking risks**!

If you want to win a match you have to be willing to take risks. The more a skill is embedded through repetition, the more calculated the risks will be. The less embedded a skill is, the less calculated (more luck than skill) the risk will be. Confidence is never built upon luck. Confidence is built upon *calculated* risks! Top competition means that participants have all mastered the basic skills. The victory on the day will usually go to the competitor who is willing to take the biggest (yet calculated) risks. Sometimes the risks do not pay off, but that's why it's called risks. However, when it does pay off you will probably win! The more you have mastered (embedded) a skill; the more calculated your risks will be and the more your risks will pay off (be successful).

How do you teach someone to become a master? How do you train someone to be willing to take calculated risks?

COACHING YOUR ATHLETES TO TAKE RISKS

A FEW HINTS:

- ✓ Always **show** your athlete the **correct choice / movement** in a certain situation. Thanks to technology we have examples of amazing acts of braveness and skill from true masters. Show these to your athletes. Avoid showing your athletes failures. It might be funny, but it puts a picture in their minds they can do without. If you want to make it great, focus on the possible and the successful!

- ✓ **Focus** your athlete's energy on **seeking opportunities** for take calculated risks. Have a motto of: *go for it!*

- ✓ Your **verbal communication** should be focussed on **what to do** and not on **what to avoid**.

- ✓ **Reward** your athlete **verbally** once a risk is taken at the right time. Even when the outcome was not perfect (the movement was simply not embedded through enough repetition) it is important to empower the act of taking the risk verbally.

- ✓ Focus on what is done right and **avoid the word "don't" at all cost**! You will never teach someone a willingness to take risks when you are actually teaching him / her to avoid mistakes!

Many coaches coach their athletes to avoid mistakes. Because of this, children lose their willingness to take risks. When this happens the adventure and thrill of participating in sport is lost! More athletes are focussed on not making mistakes than they are on taking risks. Not making mistakes is good and we will have good athletes but few champions. Creating champions takes more than not making mistakes – it requires courage and a willingness to take a risk based on the confidence in oneself, embedded (through repetition) in our skills.

Most coaches actually coach mistakes (they comment on every mistake that is made). Mistakes are the things we don't want, yet most of our energy is focussed on it! Mistakes make us feel uncertain. Mistakes create a feeling of doubt and worry in our inner being. Worry is the root of anxiety. When an athlete experiences anxiety it is a set-up for disaster. Fear and worry is the foundation of illnesses. Why would we continue to focus our energy on *not making* mistakes if we can focus our energy on the skills we want to master?

> *"The only thing that can stop you is the doubt that you carry in your mind."*
>
> - Chae Richardson

Your primal focus need to be **finding the solutions for possible problems** you might see. Your focus should not be to highlight the mistakes your athletes make. Most people can easily point out a mistake. Common sense enables us to see the smallest flaw in any skill. In every technique there might be a mistake of some kind, yet it might not be a mistake at all. It might only look different due to the frame of reference in your own mind. Have an open mind! If different it doesn't necessarily mean wrong; avoid changing it! It may be so unique that this difference might eventually become the signature of a future champion!

> *If different doesn't necessarily mean wrong - don't change it!*

Coaches often use fear as method of manipulation and power. What a tragedy! How many coaches step into this trap. Not only in sport, but in life in general.

Our fear of making a mistake has grown bigger than our desire to succeed! This approach has become a tradition in the way we raise our children. It is a fatal mindset if you want to raise and grow champions. If you fear making mistakes, you can forget about living a dream. Your desire to succeed should far exceed your fear of making mistakes. Making mistakes should be a source of motivation; not a reason to quit!

Hear the words of Michael Jordan – a legendary basketball player...

> "I've missed more than 9000 shots in my career. I've lost almost 300 games. Twenty-six times I've been trusted to take the game winning shot and missed. I've failed over and over and over again in my life. And that is why I succeed."
>
> - Michael Jordan

The foolish coach: (fear-method of coaching)

× Have no clear goals before a session

× Constantly point out and correct mistakes during training

× Constantly tell athletes what NOT TO DO.

× Uses guilt / sarcasm / disappointment / anger as source of authority and feedback

× Fills athletes with doubt and fear (and gain a sense of power).

× Threaten athletes that they will lose their spot in the team or that they will lose if they continue to make these mistakes

× Always points out mistakes during feedback.

Champion coach: (Power-method of coaching)

✓ Start every training session with clear and achievable goals.

✓ Focus more on what's done correctly, instead of pointing out mistakes.

✓ Create fun by teaching through pictures and stories.

✓ When correcting mistakes, it is done by means of giving solutions.

✓ Coach by means of giving clear direction – athletes know what to do and where to go.

✓ Use encouragement and recognition as basis of communication.

✓ Fill athletes with hope and enthusiasm.

✓ Encourage athletes to take risks, explore skills and use their unique interpretations.

✓ When mistakes are made, rather ask questions regarding solutions instead of pointing out mistakes.

✓ Always point out what was good before any change to strategy or technique is suggested!

THE POWER-METHOD OF COACHING VS. THE FEAR-METHOD:

Why does the power-method of coaching (focussing on solutions and what you want to achieve) *always* work better than the fear-method (avoiding mistakes) of coaching? The answer is founded on the universal principle described in the following quote:

"We become what we think about most of the time, and that's the strangest secret."

- Earl Nightingale

The biggest reason for failure is our fear of it! We are conditioned to avoid failures and mistakes. It means we constantly think about them! When we think about mistakes it means that our mind is occupied by pictures of the mistake. These pictures send out a message to our motor neuron system which stimulates the exact muscles and nerves to complete or perform the pictures (not the opposite of the pictures!).

Science has shown that fear causes the body to excrete toxic (poisonous) endorphins. The result hereof is an immediate contraction of the skeletal muscles (flight or fight-reaction) which is 100% *what we do not want to happen*. In sport (and in life) we need rhythm, patience, sureness and faith (all of these the opposite of fear). The toxic endorphins excreted by the body (because of fear or doubt) have also been proven to be the root of physical illnesses. I suggest you read the amazing book written by Dr. Caroline Leaf with the title: *"Switch on your brain"*. Scientific proof to what was just said is given in this book!

The answer is simple. Coach your athletes by showing them the correct execution of a skill or movement. Focus their mind on correct decision-making processes. Focus their mind on effective rhythm and total control. Get them to move toward something (the goal) not away from something (the mistake). This is what I call the power-method of coaching.

EXAMPLE:

My son and I were playing tennis one morning. He was hitting his backhand into the net more consistently than he was hitting it over the net. He asked me: *"Dad, **what am I doing wrong?**"* I thought to myself: *"Say nothing"*. We continued hitting and his failure-rate remained high. Frustration crept in and with some irritation in his voice he asked again: *"Dad, what am I doing wrong?"* Without answering his direct question I simply said: *"Victor, just turn your right shoulder a little bit more towards the ball and follow through"*. Without another word or a question he did it. Suddenly his backhand flew over the net. His first reaction was: *"It works dad!"* I smiled and said: *"The key is to* *turn your shoulder and work towards the ball"*. We continued and had a great time practicing.

On our way home Victor mentioned: *"Wow, dad, I really enjoyed today's session".* I smiled and asked him: *"Why specifically do you think we enjoyed this session so much, Vic?"*

His answer: *"I had a lot of fun dad – I don't know... I was positive and not afraid like some other times."*

I told him (as it truly became my revelation in that moment): *"You know what' Vic,' when you asked me what you were doing wrong, I never told you!"*

I simply told you what to do. Had I told you what I thought you were doing wrong it would have caused you to try to avoid doing it. How does one avoid doing something? It is almost impossible. You need to know what to do instead! Rather than telling you what you were doing wrong (in my opinion) I told you what to do instead. You did it with energy, desire and passion and it worked. We had a power-training-session and not a fear-training-session son! Does it make sense?"

I don't know whether it made as much sense to him as it did to me, but it was where things really started changing. Power vs. fear. Power will always have the positive outcome!

Become consciously aware of the consequences of pointing it out to your athlete when he makes a mistake (in your opinion). How often do we hear the following during training sessions?

- o *"No, not like that! You are taking your arm back too far".*
- o *"No, you are not following through!"*
- o *"No, you are playing only with your arm".*
- o *"No, you are constantly on your back-foot," etc.*

I can continue giving you dozens of examples of verbal methods of fear-coaching. They will all sound OK to us. We are so familiar with this method of speaking (coaching) that we don't recognize the consequences. What you focus on is where your body will go. Speak words where you want your athletes to go! It is foolish to tell your athlete not to do something!

Become a coach who can see beyond the mistakes. Become **a coach who can see the solutions!** Focus your athlete's attention on the solution not the mistake! Teach your athletes to ask: "*Coach, what do you suggest I do?*" Compare it to the traditional question of: "*Coach, what am I doing wrong?*" I am sure that you are smiling at this moment. How many of us step into this trap of fear-coaching instead of power-coaching? Any fool can see a mistake. It takes wisdom to find solutions to those mistakes.

Coaching is an adventure of discovering methods, techniques, strategies and ways to master challenges in sport and in life. Catching someone doing something wrong leaves a sour taste in everyone's mouth. Coaching should be a thrilling, inspiring and fun experience. Athletes need to look forward to every session. You need to experience the satisfaction of growth every day – achieving small goals, knowing that you are moving closer to your dream, step by step. If it is not the case, perhaps you focus your coaching too much on finding mistakes and too little on providing solutions! Ponder upon this...

7.

DO YOU KNOW WHO YOUR ATHLETE IS?

It is common knowledge that people have different personality types. The most common and well-known classification of personality types is the Meyers-Briggs classification based upon a model developed by Isabel Briggs Meyers and her mother Katharine Briggs. They based their test and interpretations on the well-known psychologist Carl Jung's work. In this personality test, basically sixteen different personality types are identified, described and categorized.

Personality and the classification thereof have many variables. There are numerous tests and / or classifications that are valid and accurate. Every one of them is good, accurate and valuable for the purpose of its development. You are however a coach and not a psychologist, so which of these tests should you use? Most of these tests are protected by copyright. They can only be assessed and interpreted by a qualified psychologist. Most of them take a lot of time to complete. The result: Most coaches never consider finding out with whom they are working. To be a real coach, you have to understand the psychological make-up of the people you are working with! You can never avoid the area of psychology when dreaming of becoming a real coach!

You might wonder: *"Do I need to become a psychologist before I can be a real coach? Do I have to hire a psychologist to asses all my players and teach me how to deal with every one of them individually?"* It would be fantastic, but what is the chance? Due to time, financial and professional constraints we put it aside. We try to forget or ignore the responsibility.

This is probably one of the most important aspects of being successful as a coach. You have to **know with whom you are working before you start!** The pain of discipline is far better than the pain of regret. A little more effort in the beginning of this journey will save you a lot of heartache and sorrow in the long run. It will enlarge your experience; it will challenge you to become more. It is exciting and energizing once you understanding how people think.

I once had a conversation with one of the top tennis coaches for women in the world. He made the following statement: *"I have to know exactly where my player is. I have to know her monthly menstrual cycle because I have to treat her correctly! If I am unaware of things like this it might cause irritation, anxiety and before you open your eyes you have lost the heart and the trust of your player. Knowledge of things like this might mean the difference between a grand-slam title and a first-round knock-out."*

Evaluate and discover the personality types of your athletes. It will make you far more effective as a coach. The first question is: *Which test do you use*? Do you appoint a psychologist and get a theoretical description of each athlete? What will it mean to you? What will you do with it? How many coaches have the financial resources and the access to such a luxury? It would be great to be able to do it professionally, yet we know that less than 1% of coaches will do it.

Regarding the question of which test to use; it doesn't really matter! What matters is that you know and understand who your athletes are! Time is always a factor. Few sport coaches have theoretical sessions with their athletes. The reason: it is uncomfortable and out of the norm.

What happens when a new athlete joins your squad after the initial start of the season? How will you know who he is? **You have to make personality profiling standard practice in your coaching**. After the initial coaching agreement the athlete needs to complete a personality profile. You have to know with whom you are working.

During my years of study we worked through quite a couple of personality tests. Every test has its requirements and every test takes time. Most people (especially in coaching) believe they don't have the time. Since starting my own practice in 1994 I realised there is always place for a test – especially if you want to understand the person with whom you are working. A test gives people a kind of security / belonging / comfort. In a coaching relationship this safety is beneficial, especially in the beginning of a relationship.

My personal preference is to do things quick, thorough and not to waste time. I decided to make it easy. I took common factors from a couple of different tests and compiled my own short personality-profiler. Is it scientifically validated? No it's not. Yet it gives me quite an accurate determination of personality types. It works for me! I repeat: *"It is not a scientifically verified and tested questionnaire but you are more than welcome to use it!"*

I include it in this book. Feel free to copy it and use it for your own benefit. It is definitely better to use this profiler than to do nothing at all! I like clarity and simplicity. I re-named the formal descriptions of personality-types. I took four animals we all know to represent the different personalities. It makes it much easier to remember.

PERSONALITY PREFERENCE QUESTIONNAIRE

There are 10 rows and 4 columns. Look at the four words in each row. Choose one of the four words that describe you the best. Make an X next to it. In every row you can choose only one word. Eventually you will have 10 crosses (one in each row). It is very important to be honest as to how you truly are. You won't impress anyone by marking a word you believe to be a better quality. There is no right or better characteristics. All of them are unique and valuable. By being honest it will give your coach a better understanding of the way you perceive things and how you think.

PERSONALITY PROFILE

	Column A		Column B		Column C		Column D	
1	Sociable		Strong-willed		Self-sacrificial		Submissive	
2	Convincing		Competitive		Controlled		Considerate	
3	Spontaneous		Sure		Scheduled		Shy	
4	Demonstrative		Decisive		Deep		Dry humour	
5	Lively		Leader		Loyal		Listener	
6	Brassy		Bossy		Bashful		Blank	
7	Unpredictable		Unaffectionate		Unpopular		Uninvolved	
8	Emotional		Argumentative		Alienated		Aimless	
9	Wants credit		Workaholic		Withdrawn		Worrier	
10	Show-off		Stubborn		Sceptical		Slow	
Total	A		B		C		D	

Add up all the crosses you have in column A and write the total at the bottom. Do the same for B, C and D.

Most people will have one column standing out. Some of you might have two columns matching each other closely but we all have a dominant column. Dominant is where you are likely to go when put under pressure...

DESCRIPTION OF EACH COLUMN

Column A = The Dolphin

○ You are a people's person and you like being around people.

○ Friendships are important to you and you will do a lot for your friends.

○ You like to be recognised amongst people and it gives you a thrill.

○ You are an emotional person and you share your feelings quite easily.

○ You are lively and optimistic; however you can become uncertain if someone does not show you that he / she likes you.

○ You are a great team-player but you do not like to make the decisions. You would rather follow than lead.

○ You are extremely aware of other people's needs (emotional and physical) and will do a lot to serve people (please people).

○ You are an optimist and ready to try and do things (innovative).

○ You are vulnerable to the acceptance of others. This might cause you to do things that you would not have done on your own.

○ You might be over-sensitive for criticism and it can cause you to go into a place of self-pity.

○ You will discard rules to fit in (follow the crowd) which means that you might be susceptible to the negative influence of other people.

○ You have a tendency to feel sorry for yourself and become depressed when things do not go your way.

○ Your way of dealing with stress is by becoming a clown – you create fun!

○ You are extremely valuable in any team because you bring laughter and fun.

Column B = The Lion

o You are a confident person who believes in your abilities. You are not afraid of taking risks.

o Initial failure usually serves as a form of motivation because you like to perform and stand out.

o You will do things without being asked as you naturally want to lead.

o You are competitive by nature which might cause you to be rather impatient.

o You like rules (especially if you can apply them) although you are comfortable with change.

o You tend to be straight-forward. At times you might lack diplomacy because you like keeping to the rules. Other people's feelings are usually less important than keeping to the rules.

o You tend to excel because of a good argument and in your opinion it is a good way to move forward in a relationship. Other personality types usually interpret a good argument much more personal and negative - be aware of it!

o You like being right. Sometimes being right might cause you to be blind to the emotions and feelings of others. Learn to have an open eye! You can only win. Relationships are eventually more important than to be right all the time!

o You like being in control. This might cause you not to listen to others. The most important skill of leadership is your ability to hear!

o The Lion loves to lead, so leadership is part of your life.

o The Lion-personality tends to be more mentally tough. You do not take things as personally as the other personality types might.

Column C = The Tiger

○ You are more than likely a very talented and gifted person.

○ You tend to be hesitant, safe and correct. You tend to think things through before you act.

○ You are focussed and better at working on your own. Working in a group might frustrate you because of other personalities' desire to socialize.

○ You are a thinker and have high personal standards of excellence.

○ This might cause you to become too critical towards yourself. It might result in you selling yourself short all the time. This often leads to a weak self-image.

○ A Tiger is someone who might back-out because you want to do everything perfect. You tend to over-analyse things so much that you never enjoy the thrill of making mistakes and gaining experience through the mistakes that you make.

○ You tend to take critique very personal. It makes you a challenging person to work with – because you tend to take everything personal! Relax more – everything is not personal. Allow yourself the freedom to make mistakes. It will enhance your relationships and relax you much more.

○ Because of the high standards you set for yourself, other people might feel insecure and inferior in your environment. This might result in you becoming a loner.

○ The consequence of this is that you might easily get depressed and feel sorry for yourself (because of lack of relationships). Work hard on your relationships and learn to respond with fun and joy!

○ You tend to think – not speak. This makes you a great challenge in relationships because you assume others know what you think. You expect others to think like you and they don't!

- You want recognition and you thrive on it, yet you don't like the lime-light. What a good challenge!

- You are led by your intuition and not by your heart and you are usually right.

- You might frustrate other people because you often lack taking action – you think and plan, but you don't move.

- Have more fun, forgive yourself more, relax – not everything is about you personally! Allow other people to make mistakes. Life is not only black and white – there are many other colours to enjoy.

Column D = The Elephant

- You are a trustworthy person who will stand by others through thick and thin.

- You avoid confrontation with everything in your being – you are a giver, not a taker! You are a peace-maker, not a fighter!

- You are an extremely valuable team-player because your biggest desire is to see others succeed. You do not care about the lime-light (you are almost shy), yet you thrive on recognition!

- You have persistence and you are thorough; when others quit, you will continue.

- You don't want to lead but when you are told what to do; you will not stop before you have done it. You are extremely loyal.

- You like structure and are not comfortable with change. You like to feel safe and security and comfort are high priorities in your life.

- You may have a weak self-image because you are very dependent upon the opinions of other people.

- When someone challenges you to move from your place of comfort to embrace an adventure, your first reaction will be to withdraw. This might cause you to not experience the thrill and the adventure of life which is available to us all.

- The Elephant personality is someone who gets to the end of his / her life and often wishes to have taken more risks.

- You rarely do something out of the norm. You are almost predictable!

- You take critique very personal and may often feel sorry for yourself. You are rather dependent upon other people to make decisions and to move forward in life.

- You are comfortable in relationships and accept other's behaviour without judgement. You avoid confrontation!

- You will often find that people abuse your easy-going nature. You might also be the one that was bullied at school because you tend not to react to confrontation.

- You might cause frustration in your relationships because you lack drive and passion – you don't move, you idle and play it safe.

- You are a GREAT team-player and essential to any team.

It is important to remember that few people are rigidly only one personality-type. We all have variations of the different personalities. We are all truly unique! The human being likes to label himself because it gives us a form of belonging and safety. If you understand and value these unique differences in people, the adventure of coaching will become a life-time memory.

8.

MOTIVATION – HOW DOES IT WORK?

The word motivation is probably one of the most used words in our language, yet one of the terminologies of which we understand the least.

WHAT DOES THE TERM MOTIVATION REALLY MEAN?

Motivation is defined as the internal and external factors which stimulate a desire within a human being to be committed to complete a certain task, action or goal.

Motivation is the result of an interaction of both conscious as well as unconscious factors i.e.

a) The intensity of a desire;

b) The value or reward associated with completing the task, action or goal;

c) The expectations of valuable others like family and friends.

These factors are the reason why we act in a certain way. Take for example the reason why a student will put in effort to get good marks. It is probably motivated by the desire to have a successful career plus a desire to be meaningful and important amongst his peers plus a desire to please his parents and make them proud. All of these factors then are responsible for his level of motivation.

Then we find the term: ***Performance motivation***. This term is used to connect certain personality-traits as well as socio-economical background issues (i.e. place where someone grew up, birth-order, socio-economic well-being, parents' history, school, etc.) to someone's desire to be successful in competition.

There is a never-ending list of components influencing an individual's motivation as character-trait as well as his level of motivation in a specific moment. Your aim is to find the best way of working with a specific individual - to raise and maintain his level of character-motivation as well as his level of performance-motivation to the maximum. ***To lift someone to an optimum level of motivation during competition is a true skill and one of the primary goals of coaching***. Optimal motivation / activation is a dynamic process which may differ from day to day and competition to competition. It remains the challenge for every coach. It is the dream of every **athlete**: To be able to raise his / her motivational-level to the optimum (best place) for that specific day, that specific moment and that specific competition.

How do you identify an optimum level of motivation? What does an optimum level of motivation means? In the earlier years (unfortunately it is still the truth for many people today) it was believed that the higher the level of motivation / activation before competition (the more psyched up someone is), the better the performance. If we draw a graph to illustrate this theory, we need to illustrate the relationship between performance and level of motivation / activation:

Note: This was the belief for many years but it is wrong...!

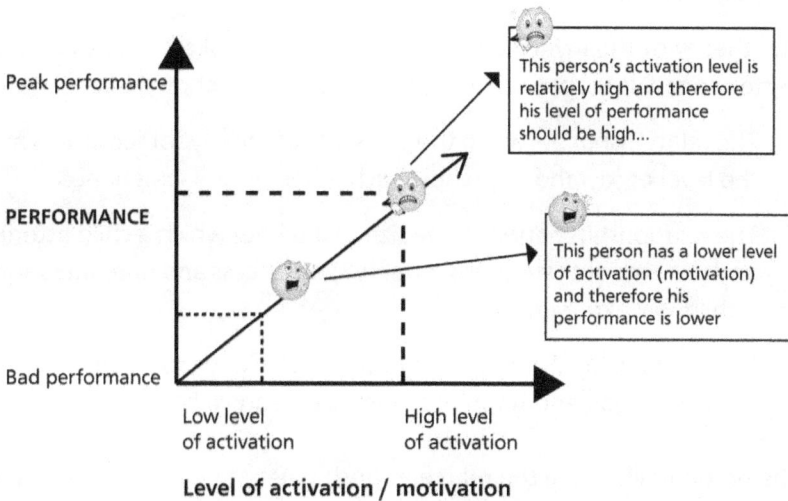

Level of activation / motivation

As research continued it was found that the relationship between the level of activation and performance is not a straight line going up. It is in fact in the shape of an inverted U! Understanding of the complexity of top-performance has increased dramatically. The uniqueness of every individual, the perceived pressure of every situation and the environmental and psychological factors present at a certain moment all has a dramatic impact on every athlete's performance. It is a fascinating challenge to understand it all.

The development of the theory of the inverted U-curve to describe the relationship between performance and level of activation is truly revelational. The theory states that there is an optimum level (perfect level) of activation for every athlete at a given point in time to achieve top performance in that moment. This level of activation is not a fixed or pre-determined observable fact. It is dependent on the changes in environmental and psychological factors in any given moment or situation. The foremost understanding that needs to be taken from the inverted U-curve-theory is that an athlete can easily be over-activated (over-psyched-up / over-sensitive / over-motivated) which will lead to a drop in performance! In common language we say that the athlete was psyched-out.

The theory of the inverted U-curve is not only applicable to sport and performance. It is applicable to almost every aspect of life i.e.

✓ The relationship between the amounts of money someone has and the level of joy and happiness such a person will experience.

✓ The relationship between the size of a school which a child attends and the amount (standard, quality?) of success and happiness such a child will experience.

✓ The relationship between the number of friends someone has and the level of joy and happiness such a person will experience.

The graph to illustrate the real relationship between performance and the level of activation / motivation looks like this: (Note: You can place any other factor - like the amount of happiness on the Y-axis and the size of a school on the X-axis, etc)

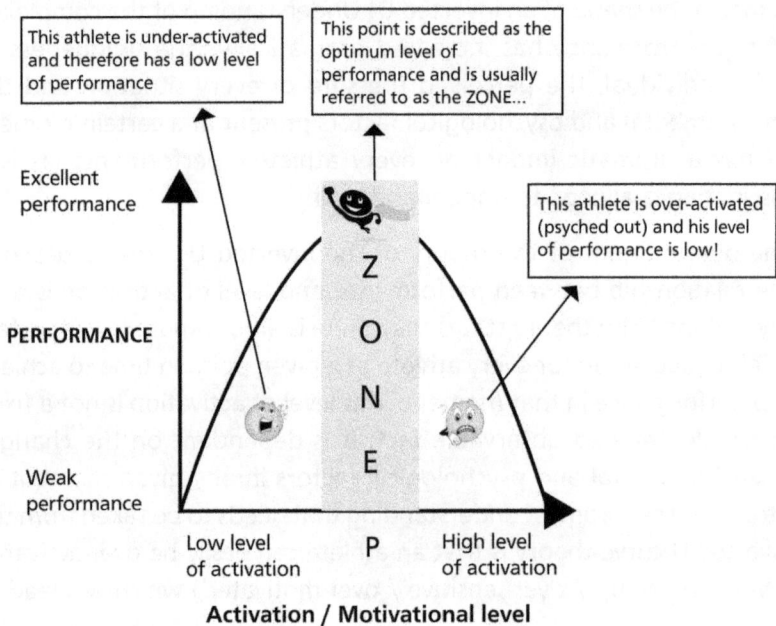

This athlete is under-activated and therefore has a low level of performance

This point is described as the optimum level of performance and is usually referred to as the ZONE...

Excellent performance

This athlete is over-activated (psyched out) and his level of performance is low!

ZONE

PERFORMANCE

Weak performance

Low level of activation

P

High level of activation

Activation / Motivational level

WHY IS THIS INFORMATION IMPORTANT?

You have to understand that every athlete needs to be motivated and dealt with according to his / her own unique personality and state of mind.

When an athlete is under-motivated / activated he will have a poor performance. This often happens when an athlete is over-confident and under-estimate the abilities of his opponent. It often happens to youngsters who are arrogant regarding their performances. They are not mature enough to understand that success and victory is a much bigger responsibility than failure.

Over-motivation (psyched out) usually happens when an athlete wants to be too correct (perfect) in everything he does. This is often the case amongst first-born-children or single children. They tend to over-analyse and personalise everything (take things too personal). Over-activation might also happen before a final, when opponents are deemed to be very good or where there is a large public expectation upon the athlete.

The ideal ("zone") is where an athlete is focussed and present in the moment. In the zone things happens automatically. The athlete does not think too much. It is a relaxed yet focussed place where the body and the mind are in sync (trust). Things almost happen in slow-motion. Athletes will testify that it was not difficult to perform at all. It felt easy.

The adventure of coaching is finding the zone. You have to find what makes an athlete tick. You need to manage adrenalin and energy. There is a magnificent book ("The Five Love Languages" by Gary Chapman) which will assist you tremendously in understanding how certain people think and act. This book is a great tool to enhance your psychological ability to be effective with your athletes.

MOTIVATION BEFORE COMPETITION:

KEY ELEMENTS OF MOTIVATION:

○ **More athletes** are **psyched out** before competition than athletes who step in the trap of under-motivation.

○ When your athlete's **chance of success is about 90%** (easy competition) you have to **stir up** emotions in terms of personal goals and dreams. The goal is bigger than winning – it is mastering a dream!

○ When your athlete's **chance of success is about 10%** (difficult competition) it is often necessary to release the emotional tension by focussing on specific, reachable goals / tasks. The thought of winning makes it difficult because of the low expectation or chance of success. Mastering simple steps (skills) must be the aim. This adjusts the difficult (winning) into something more easy (a single technique / skill).

○ When you enter a **50-50-competition** (usually a final or a competition where your athlete is equally matched) you need to read your athlete correctly. Early experiences of success in such a game are essential for continued motivation, confidence and belief. Early experience of failure in such a competition might break the athlete's confidence, motivation and belief. It might cause a fear of failure to manifest. The result is either wild, uncalculated risks (try to be lucky) or a lack of courage where the athlete tries to make no mistakes. You will never win without some kind of courage!

In this situation you set specific short-term goals not connected to outcome! In a tennis match it will be something like: *"In your first service game – aim your first serve to the back-hand of the opponent with 80% power and a high kick. On the second point – do a 90%*

power-level serve into the body of the opponent. On the third serve, go for an ace. Whatever happens after your serve is in is okay. The major goal is finding your rhythm and getting the "feel" for the ball. In your opponent's first service game, your first goal is to make him play another shot. If he has played one, make him play a second and a third."

These are simple and achievable goals. They are not focussed on outcome – it is about getting into the process (finding rhythm, seeing the ball and managing your power). **Focus your athlete's attention on achievable tasks; not a result!**

Once your athlete has mastered a couple of simple goals his focus needs to move towards a feeling of control and rhythm. When feeling good / relaxed / in rhythm / strong / in control / focussed, etc. is the goal, the right-side of the brain (creative side) is put into control as all these feelings has to do with movement of the body. If the focus of the athlete goes to technique or analysing mistakes (critical thinking), the left-side of the brain is stimulated. Free-flow movement of the body is blocked by too much analysis. Trust and confidence opens the neural pathway to free-flow movement. Critical and analytical thinking leads to doubtful and forceful movements. To move into the zone an athlete needs to be in the feeling-good part of the brain. In the zone you don't think – you feel!

During practice sessions we usually think about what we do. The coach speaks so we have to think! During competition analytical thinking needs to be limited. During competition you need to perform what you have practised. The skill-level of an athlete will obviously influence his ability to move into the zone. It is rather difficult for a beginner to enter the zone because skills are not mastered yet. A beginner still thinks about every part of a movement. The higher the skill-level, the less an athlete needs to think and the bigger the ability to move into the zone.

○ **Develop routines**. Routines act as anchors where your athlete can "re-set" in moments of intense pressure. When temporary doubt creeps in, the routines (anchors) are the way to get back into the game. Pressure or mistakes usually cause an athlete to become hasty. It is the first move to lose rhythm. In sport (and in life) everything is about rhythm. We need to "swim with the waves and not fight the waves".

Sometimes an opponent *zones* (everything just goes well). When this happens there is no use panicking. Identify the situation and focus on turning the momentum. One needs to be patient and focussed to turn momentum. Find the smallest measure of success and build on it!

Routines are actions we can control. It is things like the pace you walk, your method of breathing, what you look at, what you decide to think, walking to your towel and removing some sweat, dancing on your feet, etc. World-class athletes are known for their particular routines (anchors). It is where and when they have total control. It is their way to remain grounded. Whether they are in control of a match or whether they are in trouble – they ground themselves by performing their anchor-routines. Some athletes are more aware of their routines than others. Never allow a routine to become an obsession. An obsession is a sign of weakness!

✓ **Keep the long-term goal alive**. Children often lose motivation in the face of short-term failure (losses). It is imperative to engrave this thought in your athlete's mind: *"**Success is a journey – not a destination!**"* The biggest legends in history have amazing stories to tell about their failures and disappointments. The key is to live the dream – not the results! Failure (to win matches) is a huge reality in the lives of our heroes. Much more than most of us believe. The fact that they never quit after failure is why we are more aware of their successes - they never stop!

✓ **Make sure that your athletes always win.** How is this possible? Winning is a mindset (and so is losing). If you can create a winners mindset it is definitely possible to always win...

THE WINNER'S MINDSET:

I am a born champion
Therefore I always win
When I do not win the match – I win experience...
This experience is essential for me to
Eventually become a true master....
I need to understand what winning truly is
I need to learn to value opportunity
I need to grab every opportunity
This is my life and my adventure
This is my journey in becoming a true master
I have been born a champion
Therefore I know that I always win...

→ **Self-critique and self-judgement** is a big reason for failure, loss of confidence and a loss of motivation. No athlete will ever make it if he is his own biggest enemy. A critical spirit is like a death wish. Self-judgement is the beginning of excuses, illness and injury. Avoid it at all cost! It takes away the fun. It robs an athlete of his courage and it robs everyone else of the thrill of competition. You can never help someone who has given up! **Provoke humour, have fun, reward courage and make a huge thing of a positive mindset!** This needs to be done according to the maturity level of your athletes. Athletes need to understand humour, forgiveness and grace. You can never sacrifice discipline just to say that you had fun. Real fun only exists in the presence of discipline, not the lack thereof!

→ **Create a tradition of seeing the good in things.** Before every training session your athletes have to share something that is good in their lives. This "attitude of gratitude" is not something which happens automatically – it is a habit we consciously to create! Life (the news we hear every day) is taking care to create the opposite (worry and concern) of gratitude and faith!

→ **One of the biggest sources of intrinsic motivation is the picture of a dream.** Build your own dream-chart (goal-chart). Inspire your athletes to build theirs! A dream-chart is pictures and photos of your ultimate things i.e. the house you dream of, the teams you want to play for, the cups you want to win, the places you want to go, etc.

→ **First thing after a match where your athlete has not won** is empathy – not sympathy! Empathy understands your athlete's disappointment. Sympathy feels sorry for your athlete. *Never feel sorry for anyone!* It opens a door to lack of responsibility and self-pity (a dreadful pit of despair!). Acknowledge disappointment and build on the fact that experience was won. Take what is necessary from the match and move on. Not winning a match is always part of this journey. We have to learn to deal with it promptly and wisely.

→ **When things go wrong** it is imperative that your athlete learns to take control, make a plan and deal with the situation at hand! Blaming the uncontrollable i.e. the weather, the referee, the spectators, etc. is NEVER an option! No real champion ever needs any valid excuse. All the valid excuses of those who lost are actually integral parts of competition we need to master in order to win. Take responsibility. Learn the lesson and move on. Never go to the place of self-pity.*Self-pity is the breeding ground for arrogance, lack of responsibility (irresponsible behaviour) and quitting*. There is a solution to every challenge in life!

To motivate an athlete is vastly more than psyching him up. True motivation is your ability to trigger the correct thinking process which will ignite your athlete from the inside. The strongest source of this intrinsic power lies in the clearness of the dream. In the beginning of a coaching relationship it is imperative that you get your athlete to sell himself (his dream) to you. Once you he has convinced you, you have his conviction. His conviction is your key to his motivation! You won't have to threaten. You won't have to shout. You won't have to punish and you won't have to fight. You won't have to convince and you won't have to beg. You will simply remind him of his astounding dream!

9.
FATIGUE :
IS IT MAINLY A MINDSET?

Whatever we believe, we will prove to be true...

If you believe something is difficult, it will be ... for you!
If you believe you are tired, you will be!
If you believe something is hard, it is ... for you!
If you believe a distance is far, it is ... for you!
If you believe you are ill, you will be ... (and your body will produce the symptoms you believe you should have, to prove your belief correct!)

Our minds are extremely powerful. More powerful than most of us believe it to be. You can literally astound yourself with your abilities once you learn to control your mind!

I want to start with a couple of mindsets we've grown up with: Unfortunately most of these mindsets are "LOSERS' MINDSETS"

→ Training is difficult.

→ Training is hard work.

\

→ To become a champion is extremely tough and only a few people make it.

→ Success is generally based on how lucky you are and whom you know.

→ When I fail I am a loser.

→ If I give my best and I lose, it means I have reached my ceiling (limit).

→ Discipline is something every coach needs to enforce. Without discipline no coach will make it.

→ When an athlete holds back a coach has to punish him by means of extra physical exercises. It will motivate him not to hold back in the future. Even better – punish the whole team with extra exercises. It will make the athlete feel guilty and get him to never do it again. It will also build team spirit!

→ The harder you train, the better you become.

Imagine we change the above-mentioned "loser-mindset-statements" into the following (feel the difference as you read this)

✓ Training is a privilege and a joy.

✓ Training is part of being excellent. It is something you do with pride!

✓ To become a champion is available to us all, chosen by a few.

✓ Success is the result of excellent work, a strong mind and giving it your best!

✓ When I fail, I win – I win experience which makes me better tomorrow!

✓ When I give my best and fail I am excited because I still need to learn more. Once I learn more and am able to beat the best, I will become the best!

✓ There is nothing as sweet and awesome as the taste of self-discipline.

✓ Every true champion is motivated by the clearness of his dream. The job of a coach is to encourage and remind him of it.

✓ The better I train, the better I become.

FATIGUE... IS GENERALLY A MINDSET!

If a child (athlete) have to choose between the following options, which ones would they naturally choose? Which are attractive to the human mind?

- ○ Few exercises or many exercises?
- ○ Many laps of training or fewer laps of training?
- ○ Difficult training or easier training?
- ○ Lots of work or fewer work?

The way our minds think determines the way our body reacts. Instead of doing a lot, rather do less! Instead of making it difficult, make it easy. The human mind is always attracted to do less work rather than doing more work! It is part of human nature. Less work is more attractive and less exhausting to the body (and mind). How do we do less if doing a "lot" is essential for growth and developing physical endurance? It is rather simple...

a) **Count less!** Instead of counting every repetition and adding them all up to make up a large number of exercises, find a way to put repetitions into sets. Set your goal (and mind) on completing a few sets instead of a large amount of repetitions i.e. Instead of doing 100 push-ups; rather do 5 sets of 20 push-ups. Setting your mind on 5 sets is far less exhausting than planning to do a hundred push-ups! Instead of swimming a 100 meters by doing 2 laps in a swimming pool (of 50 meters), count it as one lap only (going there and back is equal to one lap). Instead of planning to swim a hundred lengths, it is far more attractive (to the mind) to rather swim fifty lengths (even though they might be longer). The mind counts the numbers, not the distance!

b) **Start at the end and count backwards!** Moving towards a large number causes us to feel more fatigued the closer we get to the large number. The mind counts the numbers. The larger the numbers, the more we have done... and the more fatigued we are. Change it around! Start at the end! Work backwards. Start at the biggest number (the goal for your session) and count back towards one. The energy associated with a small number and the adrenalin released knowing that you are almost at the end, increases the quality of the exercise and you master the fatigue factor naturally!

c) **Build up credit!** Some athletes want to work harder and do more than others. Instead of simply doing more and feeling that you have given more than the others, rather build up credits and gain more than the others! There is nothing physical about what I just wrote. This is all mental! Once the athlete reaches zero (the beginning) and he decides to do one extra, he counts a +1. Anything you have in the plus is a credit to you! You have not given more, you were credited with more. You gained more! You did not lose (give more) by doing more – you gained extra by applying your amazing attitude!

d) **Always beat the exercise.** Every athlete aspires to have a strong self-image, confidence and courage. Do our coaching techniques promote a strong self-image, confidence and courage or are we blinded by traditional training methods to miss seeing that we actually do the opposite? Instead of building confidence we actually break it. Instead of building a strong self-image, we allow doubt to grow. Instead of developing courage, we promote conservative behaviour. Traditionally we do exercises and training with the aim of stretching (breaking) our athletes. We assume that we teach our athletes that we will find their limits and then we stretch them to go "beyond" their limits. What we don't see is that we truly break more youngsters spirits than stretching their physical limits. Stretching someone's limits sounds perfect, but is it truly? Is that place (going beyond your limits) not invented to take place after an athlete has mastered techniques, gained some experience and matured in his thinking? How can we stretch the limits of a young child before a true love and understanding for the sport is embedded and before techniques are mastered? I believe we are breaking more athletes at a young age instead of helping them grow and develop!

We cannot truly motivate our athletes. We have to encourage them. Motivation should come from within, not from without!

A coach should not take the responsibility to set goals for his athletes – the athletes should set the goals themselves. A coach only has to guide the inexperienced athlete to set proper goals and he should encourage the experienced athlete to reach his goals!

During any exercise (especially when working with youngsters) make sure that your athlete "beats" (master) the exercise! The quality of the exercise is principal in building confidence and pride. Once the quality of an exercise drops, we accept average as good enough. The moment average is good enough, pride disappears. When there is no pride we develop a losers' mindset. Never go there! Quality of the exercise is the first priority. We first build a winners' mindset, and then we stretch our limits! We don't stretch our limits and hope to develop a winners-mindset! You will lose more athletes than you will win!

EXAMPLE:
(GOAL OF THE TRAINING SESSION IS TO INCREASE FITNESS)

Traditional (foolish) coach:

"Ok team, today we really have to grind it out! We are going to do fitness training. If you want to be the best team in the league, you have to be the fittest team as well - do you agree? We are going to do thirty two-hundred-meter sprints with little rest in between. I trust you are up to it! Let's see how well we can do it!"

Here are the facts: There are twenty players taking part in this practise session. They are all different. They weigh between 80kg and 120kg per player. Some are forwards, some are backs. There are a vast variety of differences between them all. The bottom line is they are all different! They also think different about this whole exercise. Their first thoughts about this forthcoming training event are different!

> *As you think – you are..!*

Here is the mindset of only two players:

Player A (120 kg prop): "Shucks, I am dead. I hate this. My shoes really do not feel good, it feels like I have a blister developing ..."

Player B (80kg winger): "This is going to be an easy afternoon. I will be in front and I know the others will suffer. I will look good because this is easy. No real sweat. I am in control."

The same training session will be a total different experience for these two players. Player A is broken by the exercise. He needs to be motivated and encouraged by the coach and his team mates to endure to the end. Tradition makes us believe that this scenario generates great team spirit. It might contribute slightly. The truth is that player A's spirit and confidence is broken. He feels like a loser. The reason: He is never in control of the exercise. He is constantly fighting the exercise. The exercise (in his mind) is his master! All he experience is suffering. He can't focus on doing a quality exercises – his focus is on survival! Not for one moment did he believe he will master physical endurance. His mindset is just to make it through the session irrespective of the quality of his efforts!

Player B is on the other end of the continuum. He thrives because he measures himself against players with the likes of player A. Is this not foolish? He might believe he is a master, but is he truly?

Total (wise) coach:

Coach: "Ok team – your dream is to be the top-team in the league this year. What do you believe we have to do to get there? Just consider our fitness for a moment. Would anyone like to tell me?"

Players: "We have to be the fittest team, coach – fitter than any other team."

Coach: "Would you like to work on your fitness regularly?"

Players: "For sure coach – please."

Coach: "Speed and endurance is an essential part of our physical fitness. A great exercise is doing 200 meter sprints with limited rest in between. The goal for players weighing between 80kg and 95 kg is to do it in less than 30 seconds. The goal for players between 95kg and 110kg is to do it in less than 35 seconds. The goal for players weighing between 110kg and more is to do it in less than 40 seconds... Janu, how many 200 meters do you believe you can complete successfully in this time?"

Janu: "Coach, I believe I can do at least twenty two-hundred meters in that time"

Coach: "Great! Your goal for today is fifteen, but they have to be excellent. Are you up to it?"

Janu: "For sure coach! "

Coach: "Wonderful! Fanie, how many do you believe you can complete successfully in the time-limit?"

Get every player to set his own goal. With wisdom (understanding that some players would like to impress you with their goal) assist and guide them to set quality goals and not quantity goals. Rather change quantity goals (too many) into quality goals (less but better). See how each athlete's intrinsic motivation as well as their pride sky-rocket! It is amazing! Each player has his own personal goals. These goals are characterised by:

a) Being achievable – rather less than more.

b) Producing excellence – quality builds pride. Athletes feel that they are mastering the exercise (not being beaten by the exercise)!

c) Being inspiring – the source of motivation is self-discipline - not mandatory discipline (from the coach)

As athletes mature in their self-image, their confidence and their courage, they will eventually stretch their limits (go beyond comfort). When a coach tries to stretch an athlete before he is mature enough to understand himself, you can easily break an athlete's belief, courage and confidence! Growing into a champion is a process. It takes time and wise guidance to build an athlete into a true champion! You don't do it by "breaking" him in one endurance training session.

Getting athletes to set their own goals (aiming for quality first) creates a culture of personal excellence, personal discipline and pride. Most athletes (who are serious about their careers) will eventually want to do more rather than less! The coach will never have to use aggression, anger or threats to motivate them. They will be motivated from within. All the coach has to do is to encourage and give wise guidance!

Fatigue is a mind-set we can influence dramatically! Make a few minor adjustments and move from motivation to inspiration. The process of coaching is not a one-day event. It is a process of growing with your athletes into maturity and mastery...

10.
DEALING WITH
THE ATHLETE'S PARENTS

One of the biggest challenges of coaching is probably dealing with athlete's parents in a mature and wise way. Numerous athletes' careers have been ruined due to the negative influence of their parents. Many athletes quit their sport due to the amount of pressure and embarrassment caused by their parents. Many children lose their love for sport due to their disappointments in coaches. These disappointments are the result of the fact that coaches can't be trusted to make fair selections due to the pressure from parents. Parents who have money-power and influence-power.

Numerous coaches' main source of concern and pressure are the parents of the athletes they work with. It can truly become a ridiculous source of frustration, pressure and manipulation. Coaches make decisions against their own better knowing. They select teams they don't believe in. They have to coach athletes they can't stand. Many coaches can't coach as they know they should. They have to coach in the way they are told to or are expected to coach.

I can write a whole book about the negative influences and behaviours of parents on the careers (or lack of careers) of many promising athletes. Most of the stories are too ridiculous to share. It will also cause us to look at society with disgust and shame. It is however a reality and we cannot ignore it! Parents have a massive influence on both coaches and athletes.

You need to ask yourself: *"Do I have an agreement with the parents of every athlete I work with?"*

The first step (after being asked to coach) is the agreement you have to make with the parents as well as with the athlete before you start. Without an agreement you will constantly deal with emotional pressures and issues from parents. You will most likely have to put out fires after every defeat of the athlete. The agreement you make with the parents in the beginning of the coaching relationship is essential! The effort you make with and the clarity with which you do it will save you years of concern and emotional baggage.

KEY POINTS:

✓ Are you going to be the perfect coach? NO! You are a human being and your opinions and your truths will not always be correct nor be the same as those of the people you work with. When you are appointed, you are appointed for who you are (your truths and your opinions). It is impossible to please everyone and only a fool will try to. The best you can do is to give your best in whatever you do!

✓ Parents who are present during training sessions will rob you of your authority – especially in the beginning of a coaching relationship. The more mature a relationship and the older the athlete, the more freedom you will have. A parent has the highest level of authority in his child's life. If a parent sits next to the training court / field, the athlete will always first look to see whether his parents agree with the commands and methods of the coach. *It can never work!* The child can never be sure! Uncertainty leads to hesitant behaviour which in turn leads to poor performance. Parents are not to be present during training sessions (at least not in visible eye-contact distance). The emotional energy they carry will rob any coach from coaching freely. Make it part of your agreement in the beginning! No parents within emotional-contact distance from athletes at training sessions (especially with young children)!

✓ Parents need to respect your decisions. They have to confirm your decisions with their children! The quickest way to lose authority, power and influence is when parents question a coach (in front of their children). If any athlete really wants to make it, he has to believe and trust his coach one-hundred percent. Everything is about what we believe. If children doubt their coach because the parents question him, you might as well move to another coach. Success can't be built upon distrust or doubt. Parents need to commit to edify the coach at all times before the relationship starts!

✓ Next is the parent's behaviour towards their own children. When a child arrives home and wants to complain about the expectations and behaviour of the coach, the parents have to end it immediately! You can hear and listen but never agree (unless you plan to move to another coach). The moment you agree with your child, you also agree that rebellion is acceptable and that circumstances outside of the control of your child has become his excuse for failure! To become a champion is much more than performing a skill. It is about mastering all the factors surrounding the sport (i.e. coaches, referees, spectators etc.). It is all about what the athlete eventually believes. If he believes that the coach is wrong – the athlete will never take responsibility! If your child understands that personal responsibility is not negotiable, belief in the coach will grow!

✓ Make sure that you always keep parents in the loop. Make an effort to communicate with your parents on a regular basis by means of a cell phone message. Mention your opinion / feelings / thoughts as to where you see their child. All parents are concerned and want to know what you think. They want your opinion! They want to hear that there is hope and that the effort (and money) they put in will hopefully produce favourable results! They need to hear that you believe in their child!

Be aware of this need and let them know! If you know that a child's heart is not in a sport, it is your duty to let the parents know in a proper and diplomatic way. Open communication with parents is probably one of the most important yet most avoided parts of successful coaching.

Parents can be a source of power and energy to any coach if the process is started and dealt with correctly. You have to make an agreement with the parents before you start the journey! Standing in a proper agreement will produce respect. When you falter (which we all do from time to time) the parents will cover you, not expose you! Deal with this in a proper manner and you will never have those terrible regrets of losing athletes because of their parents!

11.
HOW DO YOU BUILD A TEAM?
(TEAM-SPIRIT AND CHARACTER)

Team-sport surely is one of the most intriguing and complex challenges of coaching. A team consists of a range of different personalities put together. You have to get this versatile group to work in harmony towards achieving all the different individual's dreams as well as the team's goal all together. Team sport is totally different from individual sport. The demands of a team are far more complex than coaching an individual athlete.

There are a vast amount of theories and opinions explaining the influence of friends (peers) upon an individual. The bottom line is that the influence of a group on an individual is enormous! Group-influence also has a dramatic influence on the performance levels of individuals!

One aspect which is dramatically influenced by the presence of peers (group) is the concept of *accepting responsibility*. As individual we are responsible for the way we act, speak, practise, behave, etc. Strangely, it seems that this responsibility disappears the moment we become part of a group. Even if the size of a group is only two people, individual responsibility seems to become far less than 50% (whilst it should remain 100 %). Note that I do not say individual *effort* seems to disappear. Individual efforts are usually increased by the presence of others. The individual *responsibility* seems to disappear! I want to "label" this observable fact and call it the **vacuum syndrome.**

When a coach finds a way to minimize or remove the vacuum syndrome from his team and get every member of the team to take 100% personal responsibility, such a team will be extremely difficult to beat!

THE VACUUM SYNDROME:

This syndrome finds its existence the moment we become more than one. If you are alone on an island with no other living being present – you have nothing but personal responsibility. You are 100% responsible for everything happening to you. The moment another living being is present you become more than one... and the vacuum syndrome finds a root. The vacuum syndrome has one purpose: *To rob you of personal responsibility!*

The moment your actions and decisions are less responsible because of the presence of another being you are infected by this syndrome. You lose accountability because of the presence of another being.

This syndrome does however have a positive counter-part! The counter-part to the vacuum-syndrome is called personal responsibility. To describe the power of personal responsibility, think about the actions of a mother protecting her child in the midst of a vicious attack from an evil force. She will literally put her life on the line (take full personal responsibility) to protect her child (another being)!

The aim of coaching a team is to create full personal responsibility amongst every member of a team. Once a coach can instil this characteristic, the team will become almost indestructible or unbeatable! Think about a team existing out of members who all has the same attitude / personal responsibility as that of the mother of an infant threatened by outsiders. You can only smile. It will be amazing!

I don't want to spend too much time on the negative part (the vacuum-syndrome), because the aim of coaching a team is to create 100% personal responsibility! To understand the foundation and origin of the vacuum syndrome is however important because you have to be able to identify it as early as possible. Then you have to remove it with all your effort!

The vacuum syndrome's most fertile breeding ground is an individual with a weak self-image. A weak self-image means that a person is unsure of himself. Such a person will look for assurance (acceptance) from external sources (other people). A strong self-image is recognised by an individual who knows who he is and understands his purpose and role in a team. Such a person rarely falls in the trap of trying to impress others or proving himself. Such an individual understands that we are all different and unique and that it is okay. Forgiveness and acceptance of differences are characteristics of an individual with a strong self-image. A person with a weak self-image often displays judgement, accusation and unforgiveness.

> *A confident person knows who he is whilst a person without confidence are always wondering who others think he is*

Once a person with a weak self-image finds himself surrounded by a group (even if it is only one other person) he is usually willing to sacrifice personal responsibility to show loyalty through his willingness to conform. He does not stand for anything – he will accept anything! This individual will do almost anything to show loyalty. He sees this willingness to conform as his ticket to belong to the group. Such an individual rarely lifts the level of excellence / accountability / performance of others. He is afraid that other members of the group might see it as a personal threat and he doesn't want to create this impression. This might cause them to avoid him. To stand up or to stand out is never part of a person with a weak self-image. A person with a weak self-image conforms, fits in and stands back.

In the presence of the vacuum syndrome the individual members of the group rarely display behaviour of empowerment or excellence. The regrettable truth is that the power of a group will usually cause members of the group to engage in negative and disruptive behaviour which (in their opinion) will get the respect and support of the group. Weak behaviour will not be threatening to any of the other members of the group. Average behaviour is always safe, whilst excellence behaviour might be threatening to others. The immense power of groups is often displayed in the negative and disruptive behaviour of gangs. Look at the powerful behaviour of individuals during riots (demolishing things in the presence of others) and uproar (rebellion against authority).

Personal responsibility is always challenged in our modern-day school system. Sadly the challenge is to conform – not to stand out! Children are motivated, threatened and conditioned into the vacuum syndrome (to fit in rather than to stand out). Rebellion against authority is seen as real power (perfect example of the vacuum-syndrome). Those rare individuals who accept personal responsibility for standing up, standing out and not conforming are characterized by being discarded and avoided. They have few friends, many challenges and are often the target of bullying.

The existence of bullies (leaders of the vacuum-syndrome-infected people) is well known in society. Bullies are simply the instigators to start negative movements. Their main targets are usually those rare individuals who want to do what is right and good. The aim of bullies is to ridicule and belittle those who have the guts to stand up and stand out. The vacuum syndrome wants everyone to conform and not to accept any personal responsibility!

In sports teams you will often find that some of the biggest instigators are children with a lot of talent but little confidence (their confidence lies in acknowledgement and acceptance of a crowd). Children like these are usually spoiled rotten and may have it easy in life. On the other hand it might also be children who have a dreadful family-life and who try to avoid any attention to it. To succeed in this effort they belittle those who work hard to be successful.

If you want to find the root of the vacuum syndrome, look for children who laugh at others when they give it their best and fail. Look for those who belittle the efforts of others. Removing people like this from a team might mean that you lose some talent, but the strength of a team is not dependent upon the talent of one individual. The strength of a team is dependent upon how much personal responsibility every member of the team is willing to accept and how safe every member is in risking his best with the possibility of failing ever-present.

If a coach can teach those players with more natural talent the responsibility to inspire and enlarge the rest of the team– he will win great victories. If those players with more talent are ignorant of their role and if they live in the vacuum-syndrome (not taking personal responsibility), you will struggle to build a strong team. Everyone in a team needs to take full personal responsibility. The less the vacuum-syndrome is present in a team, the more difficult it will be to beat the team.

The vacuum syndrome is a phenomenon that is growing rapidly in our modern-day school system. Since the use of proper discipline has been ruled unlawful by the government, the door to rebellion has been opened. Rebellion is the power-source of the vacuum syndrome. There are many people present, but no-one is responsible. You don't stand out – you fit in. You conform, you accept and you shut your mouth. The rebels rule. Those who choose to live with high morals are ridiculed, pushed out and seen as weak.

Personal discipline is the foundation for authority, leadership and freedom

A foundation of personal discipline where members of a team accept personal responsibility is the ultimate goal in building a team. Without personal discipline there is no responsibility, no accountability and a huge vacuum in which people disappear! When selecting a team you first choose character. Talent is an equalizer. The character of the leader of a team is the determining factor for the direction of the team. If the leader is weak, if he conforms and if he is sucked in by the vacuum syndrome your team is doomed to a roller-coaster ride. Up and down. On the other hand - when the character of the leader is one of personal responsibility based upon a strong self-image, you have a winner!

The coach and the captain are the key-factors to a successful team. If the coach stands slave under the influence of parents or officials he will have no authority. If you lack discipline in your own personal life how can you hope to apply discipline in your team? If you conform to the pressure and expectations of friends and parents – what security will the team find in you? If you are blinded by the talents of certain individuals yet oversee their lack of commitment, your team will never trust you!

On the other hand: if you reward commitment and dedication, even at the cost of losing talent, you are building a solid foundation for a great career as coach! These are not visible things, yet they are the factors which will determine whether you will make it or not...

Respect, personal responsibility, discipline, humility, the freedom and willingness to take risks are foundational stones upon which you build a solid team. The existence of the vacuum syndrome is a cancer to any team! Every team consists of different characters and personalities (jokers, disciplinarians, talented players, loyal players, peacemakers, etc). Each character plays an essential and important role in the dynamics of the team! Personal responsibility is the "power-blanket" of successful teams!

HUMOUR IN A TEAM:

Humour is an essential ingredient of a strong team! Humour is also an important part of effective coaching. Humour has to be applied with wisdom! Certain members of a team are usually the jokers on the team. If those jokers have wisdom to know how and with whom they can joke you have another winner! It might happen that the joker of a team might be a fool (under the influence of the vacuum syndrome) which causes him to belittle the peacemakers and the talented players on the team. Many teams are ruined because of this. Nobody wants to stop a joke, but when a joke is perceived as an insult (by a certain personality) a spirit of distrust and offence is growing. This is detrimental to any team. Individual talent will then be its only strength! It is extremely important to make all members of a team aware of the difference in personalities. The jokers need to understand their responsibility regarding it!

There are rules regarding making jokes: One of them is that when you make a joke, you do it to boost someone – not to belittle them (except when you yourself are the target and you are able to laugh at yourself). Bad jokes (ridicule and belittlement) are the quickest way you lose the respect and loyalty of certain members of a team!

REMOVING THE VACUUM SYNDROME:

The vacuum syndrome finds its existence the moment we are more than one covered under the banner of a team. Because we are part of a group, people assume that personal responsibility is lost. A new identity is formed which is called a team. The question is: "*Who is the team*?"

THE ANSWER COULD BE:

a) In a powerful team: "*I am the team*". (personal responsibility)

b) In a weak team: *"**We are the team**"*
   (no responsibility – who is the "we"?)

THERE REALLY IS NO SUCH THING AS "WE".

We are all individual human beings with personal responsibility. When personal responsibility is lost, a team is weak. When an individual member of a team is afraid to make mistakes or take risks (show courage) because he is afraid that he will lose his place in the team, he is useless to the team. If anyone is afraid that his team will laugh at him when he fails, there really is no team – there is simply a couple of talented people put together thinking they are a team.

In a real team the willingness to take risks (courage) is engorged by the constructive power of the team. When a team member knows that he will be covered (backed) by his team, even if he fails, he is safe. The whole team will benefit from this individual's strength (unique talent). *How useless a talent or a skill if the person possessing it is afraid to use it!*

In a real team every member of the team is important enough (in himself) to accept personal responsibility for the team all the time i.e. cleaning up after a meeting, expressing gratitude to a host, greeting strangers or visitors, ensuring other members are informed, being on time, determining the intensity of a training session, inspiring and talking to other members of the team. The question usually is: *"Whose responsibility is it?"* In a strong team the answer will be: *"**Mine**"*! In a weak team the answer is: *"**Us**"*

In a strong team the word *"us" means "I"* = personal responsibility
In a weak team the word *"us" means "whoever"* = a lack of personal responsibility!

A PRACTICAL EXAMPLE OF THE VACUUM SYNDROME:

A sports-team stays over in a hotel. Ruben (a well-educated and sincere young man) turns into a clown. He beyond himself with excitement.

He becomes loud. Eventually he accidently breaks a window. The laughter from his friends and the lack of responsibility infuses his courage. He "accidently" overturns a bar-fridge and makes a huge mess in his room. The laughter from his team-mates only serves as source of encouragement. He tears up a bed-sheet and covers his head with it. He jokingly tries to scare the other hotel guests, believing everyone else thinks he is funny and brave. It is weird to see Ruben in this state.

Which state? Drunkenness? No – this is a perfect example of the vacuum syndrome! Ruben does not see himself as Ruben – a future Springbok-player who is committed and dedicated to his dream. At this moment Ruben is simply a member of the first rugby team of his school. He does things he will never do when he is on his own. He lost his personal responsibility. His illusion of power is hidden in the existence of the team. The question is: *"Who is the team?"* The answer in this case: *"Everyone"*. But who is everyone? Eventually the responsibility will land on the shoulders of the captain. When the captain crumbles, the responsibility is moved to the coach. When the coach crumbles the responsibility is moved "higher". Eventually this whole incident will turn into remorse and accusations. The snow-ball will continue running.

The vacuum syndrome robbed the team members from their personal responsibility. They are therefore "non-existent" as they watch Ruben abuse the power of the team. Ruben only discovers that **he is the team** when he is called to justice. He and only he is personally responsible for the damage that has been done. He will have to pay for the damages. He is the only one who gets expelled from the school – not the team!

Imagine Ruben stayed in this hotel on his own. Would he have done what he did under the influence of the vacuum syndrome? Never! How many people end up with the pain of regret after they lost their personal responsibility in the presence of the vacuum syndrome? Ask Ruben after he was expelled from his school. Ask the handsome young man in prison who got a life-sentence because he lost personal responsibility in the presence of his gang.

There is a substance enhancing the chances of being caught in the trap of the vacuum syndrome by more than hundred percent. That substance is alcohol. Once a person is under the influence of alcohol his level of personal responsibility immediately evaporates. Alcohol has the power to give you the illusion that you have the power of two or more... a deadly "team" with no single member responsible!

Once an individual is willing to give up personal responsibility because he assumes that he is covered by his team, the red lights are flickering. Many teams have gone down because of this.

The vacuum syndrome suggests that individual responsibility is lost in the presence of a team. The vacuum syndrome suggests that people will be willing to do strange things (things they never would have done were they on their own). The fact that people *assume* that responsibility is shared the moment they become part of a group is the trap in which many famous, rich and the powerful people have lost it all. In the presence of the vacuum syndrome, no member takes personal responsibility for the small details i.e. thanking a host (or the people working for him), cleaning up after the team was there, etc. These small details are the things that separate the best from the rest!

Few individuals (except when under influence of alcohol or perhaps when they have had no education whatsoever or when they are possessed by an evil spirit) will display negative or disruptive conduct in public when they are on their own (not under the influence of the vacuum syndrome). This phenomenon only exists in the presence of other human beings. A person who has an extreme desire to be acknowledged / accepted / recognised will act in a negative or disruptive manner in order to gain a feeling of being important. Acting in a positive manner is threatening to a person with a weak self-image as he is not certain whether he will truly be successful in such a deed. A negative act is however always guaranteed to be a success!

THE SOLUTION

Build a team with character, power and integrity. Build a team on the foundation of solid and clear values and principles. Make sure that your team is not infected by the vacuum syndrome. Instil *personal responsibility as a key characteristic into your team every day*. Be consistent in your expectations. Never allow mediocrity (lack of personal responsibility) to creep in. Be aware that familiarity is the first crack in the armour of a solid team. Like in marriage you have to constantly work on the small basics. Most marriages suffer because familiarity became the excuse for mediocrity.

The only way to prevent familiarity is by instilling conscious and pure practices / routines / traditions which is done daily (not weekly or monthly)! Daily practises enhancing respect, admiration, value, appreciation and self-worth is the only way a team grows in power and strength, thus removing the effect of the vacuum syndrome. The leadership of the coach, the clearness of the agreement and the consistency with which you stick to your word will determine whether the team will become a powerful unit. A powerful team consists out of individuals who all take personal responsibility for the team in any given situation!

HOW DO YOU BUILD THIS TEAM?

It all starts with the initial agreement!

A unique and special way of putting this agreement in place is to have a training-camp at the start of a new season. After your personal agreement with the team your next step is to book such a camp. A weekend away from the normal comforts we have in life – preferably close to nature where we can return to the roots of our being. When we are in nature our minds and brains has the tendency to relax and open up to new suggestions. You cannot have a successful a camp in the luxuries of our modern-day-living, where we are swamped with technology, social media, new trends, bad news, problems, challenges etc. You need to be out of your comfort zone. This will cause the athletes to be much more receptive for creative and powerful ideas.

THE GOALS OF A CAMP:

✓ To get to know each other personally;

✓ To create trust and loyalty amongst each other;

✓ To get the team to decide upon the character of the team going forward;

✓ To determine the dreams and goals for the season ahead;

✓ To get into agreement as to each individual's role in achieving these goals.

A TEAM BUILDING CAMP AT THE BEGINNING OF A NEW SEASON

Basic program of the camp:
(This is an example for a high school or senior rugby team)

FRIDAY AFTERNOON:

A formal welcome to everyone (introduce the hosts and caterers to the team). The purpose of the camp as well as the rules of the camp is discussed and agreed upon.

This agreement is done by an agreement-conversation. Here is an example of such a conversation:

> **Coach:** "Welcome to you all! I can feel there is a spirit of excitement amongst us. Before we start this camp we have to agree as to why we are here and what we are going to do this weekend. Therefore I ask you now: What do you believe is the purpose of this camp?"

Players: *"Coach, we believe the purpose of this camp is to build a team spirit and to determine our goals for the season."*

Coach: *"You are 100% correct. We have to decide what we are going to do this season. We have to decide what type of team we are going to be. We have to decide how we are going to do things... It all has to start at this camp...*

I allocated you to rooms with a specific roommate. I know it is always nice to be with your "buddy" and it is most fun and comfortable. I specifically decided not to do it that way. Can you tell me why?"

Players: *"So that we can get to know each other coach"*

Coach: *"Jip, you are right. Do you think it will work if you exchange rooms going back to the "comfort" of your known buddies? Do you think this is necessary or do you think it is not really that important?"*

Players: *"It is essential, coach, because this is the only way we are going to get to know each other."*

Coach: *"Great! Can we agree that we will accept anything else we do this weekend which may feel uncomfortable with this same spirit? It is all purposeful to the benefit of our team and well thought through. If resisted because it is uncomfortable, we lose the purpose of why we are here. Can we agree upon this? Koos, Paul, John, Andries... Francois, Allistair, Marco? (*Call each player on his name whilst walking towards him and looking him in the eye.*)

Players: *"Yes, coach, I am in".*

Coach: *"Awesome! Thanks everyone, I really look forward to an amazing weekend! All of you take your stuff and book into your rooms. We get together in 15 minutes."*

Players take their stuff and book into their rooms...

After 15 minutes everyone is sitting again.

Coach: *"We have to decide upon the character of our team. What would you like the character of our team to be like?*

Are we going to belittle each other and laugh at each other if we catch someone doing something wrong? Or would you like to be a team where we have lots of fun and jokes - but never at the cost of someone (except if it is yourself), where we protect each other, enlarge each other and cover each other? The reason for me asking this is that I have seen many teams where jokes are constantly made, but to the belittlement and ridicule of people. The effect is that team members are hesitant in their actions because they fear failure, ridicule and belittlement. They don't want to be labelled as smooth, arrogant and pushy, but it always works negatively towards any team's power. Would you rather have us be a team where we are all willing to take risks, stand up for opportunities and cover each other or do you think we should entertain a spirit of inferiority, fear of ridicule and lack of dare?

Players: *"No, coach, we would like to be a team where we are willing to take risks and where we cover each other."*

Coach: *"Great. Do you think it will work if some of us abide to the rules and others break it or do you think we should all abide to the rules we set as a team? What do you say?"*

Players: *"Coach, any rule is a rule for everyone – not only some of us!"*

Coach: *"Great. Let us write this all down so that we can compile our agreements in the end.*

Next; our discipline: (Coach brings the white-board closer and starts writing down the main points)

? *What do you think – should we be a happy-go-lucky team where we do things in an average way or would you like to be known as an exceptionally disciplined team who does things totally different from others?*

? *Do you think time is an important aspect of discipline or do you think we must have a tolerant attitude to allow members to be late?*

? *Do you think we should practice in social clothes or do you think we should have a team-gear in which we practise?*

? *How would you like to greet each other – loose and nonchalant or would you like to be known for the personal manner in which you greet each other?*

? *How would you like to be on your person (personal hygiene)? Do you think it matters what your rooms look like or do you think it has nothing to do with a spirit of excellence?*

? *Concerning training sessions – do you think we should commit to a certain level of excellence before every session or do you think we should just let it go and see what comes up?*

? *What would you like to speak during a training session – do you think complaining and ridiculing is part of what we plan to be or do you think we should commit to only speak positive and build each other up?*

? *How do you think we should leave the places we have been to? Do we leave it to be cleaned up after us or do we leave it better than we got it in the first place?*

? *How do you believe we should act when I ask the team a question? Should anyone answer on behalf of the team or should everyone answer on behalf of the team? Is it okay if I remind you about this? It will need to become a habit because we were conditioned otherwise.*

? *What would you like to communicate to your parents? All your parents are concerned about your well-being... Would you like to communicate positive energy, power and happiness or do you think it is better to remain quiet and only once something bad happens, you complain?*

? The quickest way any team steps into a deadly trap is once players complain behind the back of their coach. Players talking behind each other's back are equally poisonous to the success of a team. Do you believe it needs to be part of our team or are we going to commit today to NEVER engage in any such talk?

(In this conversation you put any possible issues on the table and address it before the season starts!)

"Great. We will get this all written down on a personal commitment declaration which every one of you will sign at the end of this camp."

Players: *"It is perfect, coach!"*

Coach: *"Tomorrow morning we start with a great training session – what time do you suggest we start?"*

Players: *"5:30am coach..."*

Coach: *"Great boys, time for supper! Our agreement starts NOW. I remind you – surprise the people serving us, clean up after yourselves and we meet again at 19h30 when we are going to watch a great movie! Have a great supper! Who would like to say grace?"*

Players: *"Awesome, great coach – we are in!"*

At the start of the film:

Coach: *"Guys, this film has a lot to do with what we are going to do and be this season. Look at what you can see behind the visible. Tomorrow we will have a conversation about the movie! Enjoy it and we see each other tomorrow morning at 5:30am"*

SATURDAY MORNING

○ Be at the field at 5h25am

○ Get into a circle and start the conversation this way: *"Good morning boys, I trust you all had a great night's sleep. I would like to know what you are truly thankful for are at this moment."* Go around the circle and ask every member of the team by his name. When the last person has finished say: *"Thanks, Chris".*

Once you have finished with the team you keep quiet... until a player asks you: *"Coach, what are you thankful for?"* If nobody asks you, you ask: *"Is there anyone who would like to ask me a question?"* It will be obvious that they should ask you the same question. This is how you start to instil personal responsibility! You don't talk if someone doesn't ask you! We are conditioned to do things because we know we should. Personal responsibility needs to be taken because it is expected. If you (coach) always take the responsibility, players will gladly stand back. Unless you expect them to take responsibility they will leave it to you to make decisions, start conversations, take control and be the only one personally responsible and accountable. Change this habit!

> Your answer to the question can be something like: *"Thanks for asking me. What I am thankful for this morning is this amazing opportunity I have to spend time with each and every one of you. I feel so blessed to work towards a dream and goal, to have an agreement with you all, to know that we are busy with something much bigger than us – we are busy with God's kingdom and His glory! I am so thankful that we are a unit, protecting each other and bringing out the best in each other. This is simply amazing!"*

Remember – whatever you speak right now is the seed of the future! The underlined words are the specific seeds I put into this conversation. When you read them again you will understand their purpose. What the players hear from you is creating a belief about what is true. Whatever we believe, we will prove to be true!

o Ask: *"Who would like to start this day in prayer?"*

o After the prayer explain the purpose of the training session. Also explain what is going to be done and the length / duration of it. Then ask: *"How would you like to do this training session this morning?*

Would you like to go full-out and give it your all or would you like to hold back a bit?" Walk to each player, look him in the eye and ask: *"Johan, how would you like to do this?"*

○ Have an amazing training session with high intensity – remember – they have not had breakfast yet! (Keep it in mind especially with the length of the session.)

○ After the training session jump into the swimming pool and have fun for about 15 minutes.

○ Breakfast is at 8am. Before breakfast ask: *"Who would like to pray?"* Then ask: *"Would you like me to ask every time or are you going to choose to do it yourself in the future?"*

9 AM – NEXT SESSION (MENTAL COACHING)

○ Start every session with a question. Start this session with a question like: *"What did you experience this morning?"* Listen to all the different experiences and then (if a player does not ask you first) you ask: *"Is there someone who would like to ask me a question?"* As soon as a player asks you the same question you answer: *"Thanks for asking me, Fanie"* (by doing this you show respect and you build respect! This habit of showing respect should eventually become a culture in your team – thanking each other for the simple things we do).

Your answer to this question might be: *"What I experienced this morning was an amazing spirit of unity and energy. I thoroughly enjoy how you all stick to your word and the agreement that we have. Thanks for how neat you left the hall last night. Thanks for being on time this morning. Thanks for your positive energy once we announced the session (which was hard)! Thanks for the positive jokes, never belittling each other. Thanks for the intensity and your level of excellence. This is truly going to be an amazing season! I look forward to this so much!"*

Once again – the underlined words are the SEEDS I sow into the minds and thoughts of my team! We call it conditioning or simply, building a belief!

○ Discuss the movie of the previous evening. Ask every member what he saw and what he took from the film into his own life.

○ After getting everyone's summary, wait again until a player asks you: *"Coach, what did you see in the film?"* Once again you thank the player for asking you and then you give your version / summary as to what you saw. What you do right now is to highlight important issues about team-work, personal responsibility, a spirit of dare, making mistakes, etc.

○ After this take a cool drink break. Before taking the break say: *"When we come back it is time to get to know each other personally."*

11н30

○ Start by explaining how important it is to know each other personally. This is an example of the conversation:

"Boys, I am married now for x years and it is shocking to know how little people know about each other. I have played rugby at provincial level for 7 years and today I know that we never really knew each other. We made jokes together, we drank together, we trained together, but we never really knew each other. The moment you really know another person you also understand why he is the way he is. You come to respect him because you know who he really is. Some of us take things far more personal than others because some of us have been hurt in our past. That hurt had an effect and if we are not aware of those important events in one another's lives, we often act in a disrespectful way without knowing it.

I would like us all to get to know each other in a more personal way. We will then come to respect each other and the camaraderie in this team will forever be a memory in your lives. I know most of you by name and by reputation, but I don't know you personally. I would like to!

I know this is not what we normally do growing up. As a matter of fact, just the opposite. We pretend and we try to prove ourselves in order to protect ourselves. If we want to be an unstoppable team, we have to do things different. We have to change the status quo!

I have messed up in my own life in major ways and I have learned many valuable lessons. I never want to let them go to waste by not sharing them.

I am going to ask each of you two questions.

1. *What is your dream in life?*
2. *What was one of the hardest things you had to deal with in your life up till now?*

I will start if it is okay with you. Francois, would you like to ask me those questions?"

Francois: *"Coach, what is coach's dream?"*

Coach: *"Thanks for asking me, Francois. My dream as young boy was to be like my father. He was a strong and impressive man who influenced others in many ways. That dream changed and eventually my dream moved to becoming a Springbok rugby-player like my uncle. I dreamt it, I trained harder than others and I was passionate about achieving it. Doors started to open and eventually I was invited to take part in the Springbok trials. An amazing opportunity!*

Something drastically happened (a story for another day) but my dream got even bigger. My dream changed to become one of the best coaches ever. I dream of becoming a true coach who one day can look back at my career and know that people were saved because of the influence I had in their lives. As coach I dream of becoming the coach of our national team one day

Francois: *"Wow, thanks coach. Second question: what was one of the hardest things coach had to deal with you coaches' life?"*

Note: Every one of us has a personal story – tell yours! Here is a version of my own...

Coach: *"Thanks, Francois. We were raised very religiously. We went to church every Sunday, I respected my parents and we were a happy family. I was naughty, but any boy should be!*

When I was in grade 8, my mother informed me that she and my dad was getting divorced. To me it was one of the biggest shocks ever, especially when hearing that my father fell in love with someone else a number of years ago. My world crumbled. My mother was crushed by this event and found her escape in alcohol. My insecurity and feelings of inferiority grew daily. I was afraid that others would feel sorry for me or that my peers would ridicule me. I underwent a personality change – I became a clown. I always made jokes, I always laughed and I was loud because I did not want people to know what was going on in my life.

I had no idea what to do. How was I supposed to act towards my dad and my mom? I even questioned the existence of God. I looked for acceptance amongst my friends and I got it by means of my ability to push my body to its limits. I trained like a maniac. My rugby career bloomed because my fearless approach made me a strong link in any team.

I was always curious about pornography. I heard that some of the boys "made out" with girls and I was curious. How? What did they do? I eventually got introduced to pornography in grade 10. Although it was an initial shock to me being brought up very conservatively, a seed was planted in my mind. I eventually got addicted to pornography. I lived a life of pretension and worst of all, I felt sorry for myself! I got married in 1994 but my marriage was a massive disaster. I cheated on my wife. I was filled with remorse and hatred. I was a total loser! We were poor and I was lost. BUT then I got saved! We were invited to attend the seminar of a world-renowned motivational speaker and pastor. I didn't want to go. I didn't have the money, but our friends bought us tickets and picked us up. I had to go... That weekend was the turning point in my life. At the age of 32 I began a new adventure in victory. I realised that Satan came to rob and destroy me and he succeeded up till then. That weekend changed my life!

Francois: *"Wow, thanks coach...!"*

Coach: *"Okay men, now it is your turn. Let's start this side. Charl, come and stand here with me. May I ask you a question?"*

Charl: *"Yes coach"*

Coach: *"Charl, what is your dream?"*

Continue going down the row. Ask every player those two questions. Every player can decide what and how much he is willing to share. Most importantly - everyone is safe because of your willingness to expose yourself personally!

When this session is dealt with in an honest and sincere way (starting with your example) it might be a life-changing session for some players! Every human being craves to be known. The world doesn't want us to be known. As a matter of fact, the world teaches us to become pretenders. Is this not perhaps the reason for the shocking number of suicides, people with depression, murders, violence, etc...?

This session is about much more than just getting to know each other. It is about building trust in one another. It can be a healing process for many players. It will only work if you are willing to share your own personal feelings and experiences in an open and honest way. If you joke (belittle) yourself in any way (because of insecurity) you might as well stop the session – it will never work!

After this session form a circle. Express your gratitude for everyone willing to take part and share personally. Express your commitment to treasure this as special and confidential. Also express the understanding that everyone else in the team will do the same.

> You can end the session in this way: *"Boys, let's form a circle. I want to thank you all for sharing and trusting us with what is important to you. I value it highly and I expect us all to treat this with respect and confidentiality. Is this okay with you all? Cobus, Charl, Fanie, Jaco, Andries, (Ask each player individually). Who wants to pray for lunch?"*

13h00 (OR ROUND ABOUT THERE) - LUNCH

At lunch you inform them that the afternoon is free – everyone can do as he wants to do (except playing television games or sitting in front of a television). Tell them there is a time-trial at 5pm. Either a 5km-run or a 10km-run. Every player chooses which trial he wants to do.

o 16h30 – Get together (all with running shoes). Explain the route (the 10km is only two rounds of the 5km). Everyone for himself! When players finish their rounds, read out their times! It is fun and inspiring! Even the players with the slowest times have to feel pride and victory in their effort. When everyone is finished – have a cool-down in the swimming pool.

o 18h00 – Start the fires and socialize. Ideal for the evening is to have a musician (or even one of the players having a guitar) singing together. A "karaoke"-facility is also a brilliant idea. For younger teams have games (two teams made up of all the even numbers against the uneven numbers) which is great fun. Games like Pictionary (not necessarily drawing but demonstration), 30 Seconds or any dynamic-fun game. Provoke competition but respect (and grace) amongst each other! Constantly guard against belittlement or offence (inflame grace and forgiveness). Create a spirit of competition bringing out the best in others... with grace!

○ After supper form a circle. Ask everyone about his experience of the day. Put two players together with the following command: *"Have a discussion about your learning of this day and end with the following question: If I can pray for you, what can I pray for? Then pray for one-another. When you are finished you can do what you want – go to bed or sit and enjoy the fire. "Thanks for an amazing day, guys!"*

22h00 – enjoy sitting around the fire and spending time together.

SUNDAY

06h30 – Get together as a group and walk into the bush. Find a spot to sit in a circle and facilitate the following conversation:

Coach: *"Is it not amazing to be part of a team where we truly know each other, respect each other and bring out the best in each other? Thanks for your stunning attitude this whole weekend and for taking part – and most of all – that you stick to our agreements!*

I notice your discipline. I notice how you treat our hosts. I notice how you cover each other. I notice the neatness in your rooms. I notice how you value our time and our appointments. I noticed that I didn't have to start every session. I see you taking responsibility for things to happen. It is awesome! As member of this team I truly look forward to an amazing season!

I want to remind you. We work towards a dream but no result can rob us from our calling! Our first purpose and aim is to be worthy ambassadors for God and to represent Him in the best way we can. We are going to be excellent in every single thing we do. I can already see how we are going to look back to this season and think: "This was one of the best of our lives!"

We all desire to grow spiritually as well as physically and mentally. Do you think we can support each other in all aspects during this season or should we just play rugby? Koos, what would you like to see happening? Andre, what would you like to see? Gert, what would you like to see?

Players: *"We would like to grow together on all levels coach!"*

Coach: *"Wonderful. How do you think we are going to do this?"*

Players: *"We have to make time for it every day coach. All of us should take responsibility for it coach"!*

Coach: *"Great! Would you like to start today?"*

Players: *"For sure coach, but how do we do it?"*

Coach: *"Joggie, read us a passage from your Bible. Let's read from Proverbs. Read Proverbs 1, please Joggie."*

Joggie reads the passage. When he is finished pair the players in groups of 3 with the command: *"Tell each other what you have heard or what you see as important in that passage. How do you see this as applicable in our rugby and how are you going to make it work in your personal life? Once you are finished with this discussion ask each other what you can pray for and then pray for one-another."*

8AM – BREAKFAST

9AM – MENTAL SESSION

Begin with praise and worship. Perhaps play praise and worship music or play a DVD with words on the screen to sing along to.

o *Begin with the question: "What do you believe are the most important characteristics of a winning team? Have a discussion, get opinions and write it all down on a white-board. Once you find that the conversation is at its end, state the following question: "I am going to summarize everything we discussed and agreed upon this weekend. I will set up a formal agreement which needs to be signed by all involved. Is it okay with you all?*

We have come to the end of an amazing weekend. I would like everyone to step forward (speaking in front of people is one of the things you have to master if you dream of becoming a master!). I want to hear what you take for yourself from this weekend and what we can expect from you as a player in this coming season..."

o *"Who wants to start?"*

Give every player the opportunity to come forward and answer. Once everyone is finished you ask: *"Is there anyone of you who would like to ask a question?"* One of the players will ask you: *"Coach, what do you take away from this weekend with you?"*

Your answer will be something like this: *"Boys, I feel thoroughly enriched after this weekend. I have a sense of anticipation and expectation within me – not only for the rugby we are going to play but also for the leaders and champions that we are going to become. I have discovered a true hero in every one of you. What I take with me after this weekend nobody can ever take away from me again! I have discovered friends and partners. I take with me a memory for life. I take with me hope for a magnificent season!*

What you can expect from me is to be open and honest with you at all times. I commit to be on time. I commit to take responsibility for the decisions I make. I commit to always be positive no matter what. I commit to make decisions to the best of my ability even though I know that some of you are going to experience disappointment at times. I commit to do everything I do as good as I can in total dependence upon God and in order to glorify His name! Thanks guys! Let's finish off this camp.

Make a circle and ask anyone to close with a prayer. Greet the players one by one with the hand and look them in the eye.

It is totally senseless to greet someone without looking that person in the eyes! Only fools do so. It is rude. You make the person you greet feel insignificant. Many coaches become so familiar with their athletes that this small and significant act became an unnecessary time-waster. The fact that you drop the opportunity to show respect and thereby gaining authority is overlooked! *It is the small acts of excellence that eventually creates the biggest gap between successfully working with people and simply having an average relationship with others.* Rather greet less people and spend a second or two more engaging in a sincere conversation than greeting the whole world but have contact with no-one! One true friend is worth far more than being known by ten strangers.

The above-mentioned camp programme is applicable for people from the age of grade 7 and up. To build a team with younger children is something different and not as formal. Their level of maturity and reasons for taking part in competitive sport is different. Too often we assume that young children have the same goals and dreams as adults. They don't! Missing it might cause you to miss them (like my son's rugby coach missed him totally in grade11).

WITH YOUNGER CHILDREN:

Their main reason for taking part in competitive sport is the fact that they can make friends and they can belong to a group. You have to remember this in your dealing with them throughout the season. Yes, you would like to create a winning culture but never at the cost of relationships and joy!

With younger children simply have a get-together one Saturday-morning. The purpose of this get-together is to get an agreement and to start a culture of enlargement and safety (as opposed to the general culture we get amongst school-children of belittlement and anxiety).

Programme:

Welcome the parents and the children. Explain the purpose of the morning. It will look like this: (Very important – make sure that every parent has a name-tag!)

"Good morning everyone! Thanks for waking up early this morning to be here on time. We have to decide what kind of team we are going to be this season and we have to decide how we are going to relate to one another in this environment. I would like all the parents to be present because they are all part of this team!"

The parents move to the back on their chairs whilst the team sits in half a circle in front of you on the ground. Sit down on a chair in front of them (in a conversational set-up).

Coach: *"I would like to ask you a question: Why do we play rugby?"*

Children: *"To win coach... to work together as a team... to become strong and fit... to..."*

Coach: *"All of you are right! The main reason why we are going to play rugby this season is so that you can all fall in love with this game. Secondly I would like you all to feel the amazing power of being part of an awesome team. I would like you all to learn how to properly tackle, catch, run and play. Some of you are going to have so much fun that you might begin to dream of becoming a Springbok one day. If you want to become so great you will have to work hard and be disciplined to get there! You need to master all the skills and very importantly, you will have to learn how to play together as a team because not one player will ever make it on his own. Are you game for this?"*

Children: *"Yes, coach!"*

Coach: *"Great! We have to decide and agree upon a couple of things this morning:*

a) What are you going to do when coach explains something? Are you going to listen or are you going to play around and not pay attention?

b) What are we going to do when coach tells you what exercises we are going to do? Are we going to complain or are we going to shout "YES, COACH!" And then go full-out for the exercise?

c) How are we going to treat each other? Are we going to fight with one another and belittle each other or are we going to be best friends and cover each other at all times?

d) What do we do when a team-mate makes a mistake? Are we going to laugh at him or are we going to immediately cover him with encouragement?

e) What are we going to do during matches? Are we going to fight amongst each other for the ball or are we going to protect each other as a team?

f) Are we going to be afraid to make mistakes or are we going to have fun and give it our best shot every match?

g) What do we do when opponents score a try? Are we going to blame one another or are we going to look each other in the eye and get back up and go and try to score a try ourselves?

h) What do we do when we win? Are we going to belittle the opponents and make them feel like losers or are we going to remain humble in our excitement and celebrations?

i) How would you like to practise? Would you like me to constantly ask you to obey or are you going to be the best part of my team making it easy for me to coach you?

Most coaches are aware of the specific challenges you will face during coaching. Coaching can become a nightmare unless you make a proper agreement! Once you have an agreement there is accountability! *Remember, an agreement is never made with a group. You can only make a proper agreement with an individual.* Once you are finished with the specific agreements ask every player to come and stand next to you. Put your hand on the player's shoulder and ask: *"Team, do you all commit that you will support and treat Jaco as we discussed - as one of your team members?"* Team: *"Yes coach, we will!"*

Coach: *"Thank you team – I appreciate it"*

Coach: *"Jaco, do you agree to commit to all the things we discussed and do you commit to be a strong link in this team?"*

Jaco answers: *"I agree, coach."*

Coach: *"Thank you Jaco, I look forward to working with you".* In this way you create personal responsibility and accountability with each player individually. (Parents sit as witnesses!)

When you are finished ask the team to stand in a circle and ask all the parents to come and stand behind their children and put their hands on their shoulders. If there is a child without parents present simply ask the parent next to him to put his hands on his shoulders (as a parent). Then pray:

*"God, we thank you that **we stand in agreement**. We commit to do all things to the best to our ability and to honour YOU! We are here for you. We will all make mistakes and we know we are not perfect and that is okay with You. We know you know our hearts and that is all that really matters! Mistakes can never rob us from Your love for us! We look forward to amazing friendships, experiencing life and living our dreams. We do this all in our total dependence upon your power in our lives. Amen."*

Let the boys go outside and play games.

The next step is a conversation with the parents. Ask them to sit close together in front of you.

Coach: *"Thank you so much for your support and being here this morning. My main purpose in coaching your children is to develop a love for this game by means of getting your children to experience success. My main aim is NOT to win the league! My main aim is to teach and develop skills, character, and friendships and to build a love for this game amongst your children. Eventually this will culminate into us becoming a winning team as well.*

My request is that you will support me in this. I will acknowledge hard work, discipline, keeping our agreements, development of skills and great sportsmanship in this team. I ask you (if possible) not to be present (within emotional distance) at training sessions. Your child will constantly look for your acknowledgement. He will be afraid to make mistakes and he will never be free to live act as an individual. It will also rob me of my authority as your child will always check whether you agree with the teaching and coaching I do. You are and will remain the most important people in your children's lives – I can only coach them if you give me permission to!

I know that I will never please everybody. I don't plan to try to either. I am not a fool. Team selections have to be made. It is not possible to choose every player for every game. Certain players will definitely get more opportunity than others but every player has a function in this team. If you trust my judgements and selections, this relationship will work magnificently. If you query and disagree with me constantly, it will never work. You have to back me with your children otherwise they lose faith in me and then we might as well stop before we start.

I would like to get to know each of you better. I believe it is important that you get acquainted with each other as well. You are going to see each other for many years at all the school games. We might as well get to know each other personally.

Can I ask you to come and introduce yourself? Say your name and the name of your child. Where do you come from and what is your occupation. Can we start from this side?"

Call the parents to the front and let them introduce themselves. Call both husbands and wives. Once they introduced themselves give them a hand (applause) and then ask: *"Fanie / Magdaleen, can I depend upon your support in the agreement I made with your children?"*

When everyone introduced themselves thank all the parents and enjoy a boerewors-roll and whatever you have available.

12.

THE TEAM TALK BEFORE A MATCH

This is probably one of the biggest traps many coaches step into. The traditional team-talk before a match meant: ***Motivate your athletes and get them psyched up!*** "Psyched up" meant that your athlete is highly energised, focussed, thinking and ready"! It is wrong!

You don't want your athletes to think too much during competition. During competition they should trust themselves and just do what they trained to do! A coach has to motivate his athlete – it is one of the primary functions of a good coach! The term motivate is probably one of the least understood terms in our language. It is something we know very little of.

I suggest we use a different word to describe the job of a coach before a match. The job of a coach is not so much to *motivate* his athlete as it is to ***aim his athlete (or team)***! You have to aim the energy (physical, mental and spiritual) of your athlete towards a specific task.

If you have a gun, your first task is to aim towards the centre of the target before pressing the trigger. Pulling the trigger will cause you to move the weapon off target (even if it is a very slight pull). If you aim at the centre of the target (the middle) the chance that you will hit the target is quite big – IF your estimation of the distance is correct, your consideration of the wind effect is correct and your basic execution of the shot (pressing and not pulling the trigger) is correct.

When a skilled shooter considers the three factors mentioned, it might cause him not to aim at the centre of the target, but perhaps a little bit higher and maybe a little right, or a little left depending on the direction of the wind. Is he 100% sure that he will hit the centre of the target? Never! It is always a calculated guess! The accuracy of your guesstimate will be determined by your previous experience. The more experienced you are and the more training you had will influence the accuracy of your guess!

Are we ever 100% sure of a perfect shot (in the middle of the centre)? Never! Every factor influencing the trajectory of the bullet causes out of control variations which give sport and competition it's character and thrill. Without these factors (which we hope and try to control as far as possible) competition and sport would lose its attraction. These uncontrollable factors are the stuff completing the idea of competition! Our aim is to master and control those factors as far as possible. In doing so, you will also compare yourself to someone else's ability to master the same factors.

When you aim your athlete, it means you focus your athlete's energy (physical, mental and spiritual) in the correct direction (taking into account all the different factors) to enable him to hit the bull's-eye with the most accuracy. It is never the same – every day is different. Every competition is different. We are human beings and we are different every day!

Considering some of the most common and predictable factors we can aim to narrow our methods down to a certain extent!

THE 90-10-GAME (EASY GAME):

Your athlete's chance for success is about 90%. If you approach an easy game incorrectly (aim your athlete wrongly) it might result in a shock-defeat as well as embarrassment to both yourself and your athlete! The biggest mistake we often make is not aiming our energy at all before an easy game. We just pitch up and think winning will just happen. Wrong! Many shock-defeats of over-confident athletes are the testimony to this fact. We can't just shoot in the dark and hope to hit our target! We have to aim! Only a fool will shoot a shot in the dark... hoping to hit his target.

In this type of match one can easily be over-confident. It might cause you to have low levels of activation (energy-levels) and, sad to say, arrogance often creeps in. We need to have self-confidence, but there is a major difference between self-confidence and arrogance. They are both spirits. A spirit of arrogance usually blinds you for the most common snares which might cause you to fail terribly. An athlete may wakeup too late to do the catch-up after falling behind early, due to being over-confident. Yes, it might happen that an athlete wakes up in time. With extreme and focussed effort he might win back the game, but it might be too late as well! The consequence is then an embarrassing defeat.

Coach:

✓ Be aware of your athlete's prediction of his chances for success.

✓ Be sensitive for over-confidence and arrogance.

✓ Aim your athlete's energy (physical, mental and spiritual) towards a very specific target.

✓ Winning is not the ultimate goal (aim) of this match but mastering certain skills and applying certain strategies are. In this scenario, the thought of winning means that the target is too big (too easy to hit). You have to narrow it down (get the target smaller). You do this by setting specific skills-goals which your athlete needs to master during the game.

✓ You might even set a target as to how quick and how efficient you want your athlete to score points. This game is not about winning but achieving far more than that!

Example conversation (tennis):

"Victor, today is a great day to prepare for the rest of this season. I would like you to apply the techniques and strategies we practised the past couple of sessions.

✓ *I want you to serve and volley. Put pressure on the opponent from the start! Most importantly – you have to make your first volley!*

✓ *When possible run around your backhand and hit that inside-out forehand!*

✓ *I want you to hit your cross-court with much more power and control. Aim to keep the opponent playing as long as possible!*

✓ *Put on the pressure and keep it there! Even if you make mistakes I want you to continue to attack. Today is a great day to do this!"*

Example conversation (rugby):

"Boys, today is that opportunity where we are going to exercise those entire skills specific to your position.

Jaco (prop), today I want to see you work from the scrum and make a big clean at the ruck. I am looking for at least two massive tackles from you in the first half. Is that OK with you?

Fanus (hooker), today I want to see you master every throw-in on our own line-outs! I want to see your jumpers smile at the accuracy of your throws. I also want to see you at the rucks – you are a wrestler and strong in your upper-body. I want to see at least two ball-steals in this game. Is this OK with you?

Charles (lock), I want to see you take control of the line-outs today, Charles. Not only our balls, but the opponents balls as well! I am looking for a big run from you – you have speed and power and I want to see you use this today. Is this OK with you?" etc...

THE 10-90-GAME:

Your athlete's chance for success is small (about 10%) and the opponents are superior in terms of experience and ability. In this scenario it might happen that your athlete gives up even before the game starts. This will cause him to have a "don't care" attitude. He will not try his best. He will often make jokes to protect himself from the embarrassment associated with defeat. In making jokes and trying to be lucky he experiences less of an embarrassment than to give his best and still not win.

Many young children experience this type of match as very negative. It causes many of them to quit sport and competition because comfort and having things easy has become part of modern-day living. For sure, no one would like to compete in a match where the opponent is far better than you. In primary schools such an opponent will often also ridicule you. It is one of the worst embarrassments in life. You need to be a wise coach to keep your athlete's heart and commitment when he engages in such a match.

THE WISE COACH:

Tell your athlete that you are aware of the advanced skill level of the opponent. You don't expect your athlete to win this match! Never fall into the trap of trying to create a false hope by insinuation that your athlete might win if the opponent does not arrive. Never build expectations on the foundation of luck. No-one can build a career or a future on being lucky especially when working with young children. Never let your athlete feel that you lost your common sense. This might cause him to lose faith in you!

There are the 30-70-games where you do have some chance of being successful. In such a game focus on the successful execution of skills which (if you are able to execute them successfully) might cause you to upset and disrupt the opponent. If you can succeed in this it might cause you to win – but not in the case of a 10-90-game!

In the 10-90-game

✓ Assure your athlete that you are aware of the skill level of the opponent.

✓ Make your athlete aware of the fact that he is at the start of his career and busy with a process of improvement and gaining experience. The result of this match is not the end of his career – it is an essential part of gaining experience!

✓ Aim your athlete's energy towards mastering one or two simple skills (nothing to do with outcome). It can be something like succeeding in hitting at least 70% of his first serves in. It can be to make one or two good tackles in the game. It can be to run full-out for the first 50 metres and then run with a high and easy-posture in athletics. Every sport has specific skills which can be used as aim.

✓ Make it clear to your athlete that you will not measure the success of this match by the outcome, but rather by his commitment and his effort to execute the identified skills.

✓ When your athlete masters even one of those skills, show your excitement and celebrate it.

✓ Make your athlete aware of true sportsmanship. Respect and effort can never be less than his best, otherwise he acts like a loser and not the winner he plans to be. If you can get your opponent to give it his best – you are a worthy opponent yourself!

Example-conversation: (Netball)

"You all know that we are playing against X today. They are the champions of last year and they are a magnificent team. We are busy building our team and we improve daily. I have no expectation that you should win today. What I do expect from you is to work together as a team, to be positive with each other and make the opponents work hard for every point they get. I would like us to have moments of fun while we try our best and even if we fail it is nothing! As long as we give it our best shot! I would like us to celebrate even the smallest accomplishment on the court.

Susan, you are fast and witty. I would like to see you being a headache and a problem to the opponents. Try to frustrate them by intercepting their throws and make it difficult for them to perform well.

Alet, you have the ability to be in the face of the opponents because you are so tall! With your long arms and the twinkle in your eyes you can get them to doubt themselves. I would like you to spread your wings so that the opponents have little space to move. When we have the ball, take your time and enjoy every throw you make! When I look at you I want to see that twinkle in the eye. Is that OK with you?

Maria, you are our goalie. I want you to do one thing today. When you get the ball I want you to immediately slow down. Take your time and aim well. If you succeed in remaining cool and calm it is going to be so much fun watching you. Can you see yourself doing it?

THE 50-50-GAME:

These are the tense games. Usually these are the games where rivals play each other or in the finals of a competition. In such a match the victory can go to either side. The emotional energy and the levels of activation are usually very high. It can often get too high (psyched out) if not managed properly. Often these games are lost because of athletes being psyched out (over-motivated). What psyched out means is:

a) Your athlete thinks too much, over-analysing everything. He looks for the slightest mistakes and eventually lose confidence.

b) Your athlete is afraid of making mistakes and plays defensively.

c) Your athlete becomes intensely aware of factors outside of his control i.e. weather-conditions, referees, spectators, etc.

d) The slightest mistake causes the athlete to become negative and this negative emotion easily starts to snow-ball.

Coach:

✓ Make sure that you are aware of your athlete's emotional state of mind.

✓ When you notice concern or doubt, remind your athlete of prior successes in his career. Remind him of a similar situation where he previously dealt with it successfully.

✓ If your athlete has not been in a situation like this (or perhaps he failed in his previous 50-50-match), refer to other athletes who dealt with similar situations with great success. Speak about the mindset of those athletes and what they had done to be successful. They focussed on possibilities and opportunities – not on fear and doubt!

✓ Aim your athlete's energy towards his strengths. Build a strategy around your athlete's strengths and not so much around the opponent's weaknesses.

✓ Make sure that there is always a plan B, and when plan B does not work – have a plan C in the pocket!

✓ With available technology it is essential to study the opponent's methods and strategy of play. This will enable you to build a plan

B and C around possible weaknesses of the opponent. Plan A is built around your own strengths. Discuss ways of neutralising any strong points of the opponent. It is an essential source of emotional strength for your athlete.

EXAMPLE CONVERSATION (ATHLETICS)

"Janco, today is what we worked for the whole season. Your preparation was perfect. All you have to do today is get into your own tunnel and run your own race. If you are good enough you will outrun the opponents. Your aim is not on winning. Your focus is your rhythm and enjoy the moment. Winning will take care of itself!

Think back to your qualifying race. What did you do? (Listen to his answer). *You are right, it was the ease and power with which you excelled and then that last rhythmic and flying 200 meters! Your endurance is your strength – you can keep a high pace longer than most athletes. If they start fast you need not have any worry. Let them pull you and when you feel like it, shift into your fifth gear and show them red lights. You are ready for this race. Breathe deep and relax. Slow everything down to a blur. When the race starts you can explode like you always do and remember – your best is good enough!"*

EXAMPLE CONVERSATION (HOCKEY):

"Girls, this is the final we dreamt of this whole season! Well done on getting here. Today we simply finish our picture for this season. We are all proud of you. I want to ask you: "What makes you such a good team?" (Listen to their answers). *You are 100% correct and this is exactly what we are going to focus on today! We are going to do what we know how to do!*

What do you think are the strengths of our opponents? (Listen to their answers and if they miss something, just add it). You are correct. We are going to focus on our strengths first! We do what makes us good, but we should also plan to neutralise their strengths.

Liezl, you are our first line of attack. Can you see yourself frustrating and blocking Chantelle (the opponent's key-player) out of their game?

Sanet, are you and Anke ready to take the attack right through the middle where they never expect it? This is what we have done the whole season. No team was able to stop us. Let's do it again girls! I want to see a sparkle in everyone's eyes. I want to get a thumbs-up every now and then (no matter what the score is) and when we make a mistake (which we will often do because of the type of game we play) we cover each other at all times! Is this OK with you? Don't think too much today – just do what you have been doing the whole season and enjoy it! I am always proud of you!"

THE 30-70 – GAME

This is a game where you play against an opponent who has beaten you before. You are the under-dog and the emotional momentum is with the opponents. These are great games because you can only win. Your aim is however very important!

Your athlete's chance for success is questionable but there is definitely a chance, if certain things fall in place and your athlete execute certain skills correctly!

Rule number one: You can never play it safe in such a game! Playing it safe is not an option! Attack, taking risks and grabbing every opportunity is the mindset! When a moment / opportunity is successfully executed, it might easily turn the momentum in the game. That is your aim – to turn the momentum. Once your opponent doubts just a little bit, it is your key-moment. Attack with everything you have. Get your opponent on the defence. If a risky move does not pay off, don't lose hope. Look for the next opportunity. There is nothing to lose! As a matter of fact, you are constantly busy sowing seeds of doubt in your opponents' mind!

Your athlete needs to look forward to this type of game with enthusiasm, dare and a kind of playfulness. You need to consciously take risks and apply consistent pressure on the opponent! If you approach this type of game conservatively your chances for success is very slim. When you play this game with a conservative mindset you usually walk away with feelings of regret and disappointment because you know realiseyou never gave yourself a proper chance.

These are those games in life where winning is the only thing. You can either win the match or you win experience. You can try everything you are usually too afraid to try in close and important matches. What a disaster if you allow a game like this to slip through your fingers because you were too conservative and afraid of making mistakes! This is magnificent games to play!

It doesn't mean that you make radical and stupid decisions – not at all! It simply means that you engage in an adventure in your decision-making. Look for opportunities. Try things you have practised. Make moves the opponent doesn't expect. Be sharp and ready all the time. Try skills you have mastered but not applied yet! This is when you do that grubber-kick close to the opponent's goal-line. This is when you take that quick-tap penalty in rugby. This is when you play that unexpected drop-shot in tennis. Take risks without fearing the mistake or the consequences. It is calculated risks! Plan for things that excite and thrill you! These are the games in which players can experience the joy and thrill of adrenaline at its best!

Coach:

✓ Make sure that your athlete knows that you don't expect him to be conservative or to avoid mistakes. To the contrary – make sure that your athlete knows that this is the game to grab the slightest opportunity and take risks!

✓ Get your athlete to look forward to this game. His mindset needs to be looking for opportunities to surprise the opponent, upset the opponent and turn the momentum!

✓ Emphasise keeping this mindset right through the match! How useless will it be if you turn the momentum by playing with courage, and once you lead, you stop taking risks and start to defend! The moment you stop your fearless attack the momentum will turn back. Keep on attacking and stay in the adventure. Enjoy the moment knowing that you live on the edge!

✓ Remain free, trust your instinct and go for the big moment! This is what life is all about. You might miss it, but what the heck – you might hit it and have an unforgettable memory!

EXAMPLE CONVERSATION (TENNIS):

"Victor, this is a great opportunity. You can only win, but you have to play with adventure! I know that X has beaten you before. You have however grown in your experience and abilities! You need to take risks today – do what he will never expect you to do. Attack the net suddenly. If it works you might just turn the momentum. The aim is to try everything we practised to turn the momentum (the opponent's mind). When you get your opponent to doubt, he will start to defend. Once he does, you increase your attack! The mistakes you make today does not matter! It is all about your willingness to take risks! If you can succeed in getting your opponent to doubt (because of your willingness to take risks) the match can turn in a second.

Most importantly, you have to come off the court knowing that you tried everything. You went for the big shots and you played free. You must have fun! Be sure about this – the best in the world *are the people who live this way. They take risks and they often fail but they understand that real success is on the other side of failing! The more you move into the mistake-zone, the more you will move through it. Once through it you find success! What would you like to try it today Victor? (*Listen to your athlete and encourage whatever he comes up with*).*

I look forward to see you go out there today not trying to defend an image, but to build a reputation! A reputation of a fighter, a challenger and an adventurer! Enjoy every moment out there!"

Remember: RESULT is something we cannot control. We can only control what we do. You can never control the performance of an opponent! The fact that we cannot control or predict the result of a match or competition with 100% accuracy is what gives competition its attraction – not only for the athlete, but also for the spectator!

It is never wise to have an outcome (winning) as your goal. Having such a goal is trying to predict the weather with certainty. Impossible! It is about what you do in the heat of the moment, in the midsts of circumstances and with all the combinations of factors influencing the moment! Trying to predict everything is boring, impossible and foolish. Preparing for everything is the challenge. Living the moment and grabbing every opportunity is the adventure. It is available to us all! Just do it!

13.

WHAT TO SAY AFTER COMPETITION

What we say and do after competition has a dramatic impact on the self-belief, the future expectations and the amount of personal growth an athlete will experience in his career.

> *It takes time to build trust and confidence.*
> *But it can be ruined in a moment...*

Coaching has much more to do with successful relationships than anything else. When an athlete believes and trust his coach, his coach can basically tell him anything and it will work (or annihilate) the athlete! Before and after any form of competition the emotional intensity caused by the uncertainty of the outcome, the bravery needed to engage in the event, the presence of challenges surrounding the event, the confrontation caused by the presence of an opponent etc. is extremely high. This is not only true for the athlete but also for the coach, the parents and the spectators.

What you say after competition can literally make or break your athlete!

Remember – your athlete has an intense desire to please you. We please other people by finding what is important to them and then we try to achieve that! Your athlete will try to find what you regard as important. He discovers it by finding your focus.

If you ask your athlete about results first his main objective will be outcome (winning)! Focusing on results and aiming to win is unwise. We have little control over what an opponent can do on the day. We can only control what we do! Outcome (winning or not winning) is the result of achieving specific tasks you set for yourself before any competition.

If you (coach or parent) don't know the result of a match or competition, your first question to your athlete should be: "*Tell me about the match you played today*". The athlete can decide for himself when or how he wants to share the result. The important aspect is that the result was not your first objective. Your first ambition is the athlete and his interpretation and experience of the game!

HERE ARE SOME EXAMPLES OF CONVERSATIONS WITH ATHLETES:

a) After suffering defeat
b) After being victorious

Note that you can have these conversations with both an individual athlete and a team. In a team set-up you will address the whole team and even get more than one answer on your question.

If there was a draw in a match / competition you have to distinguish by "reading" the mind-set of your athlete. Did he experience this draw as a defeat or a victory? Then act accordingly!

A) AFTER A DEFEAT:

Your athlete will surely be disappointed. Acknowledge and applaud his disappointment. Not recognising disappointment might alienate you from your athlete. Feel with your athlete, but never feel sorry for him! Acknowledge disappointment first by mentioning that you are glad to see that the competition was important to him. The athlete needs to understand that you are not disappointed in him as a person. You value him as a person, yet his effort or decision-making might be better. You have to (emotionally) build your athlete first!

Your first response: *"I understand that you are disappointed and I know the feeling – I have been there many times myself. We often wish that we could have a moment over. I am so glad to see that this is important to you. I want to tell you that no matter what – I am proud of you and the effort you put in. We will learn from this and move forward..."*

After you have dealt with the negative emotion accompanying defeat, you need to get your athlete to talk about any form of success that was achieved. You do this by asking questions! Success is possible to anyone who set wise goals before competition. Success remains our biggest source of motivation. If you set simple and achievable goals before competition, the chance of your athlete achieving one or two of them during the match is highly likely. First focus on this! Celebrate any form of success before you start to analyse and give learnings.

Your first question: *"Which of the goals we have set before the match did you achieve?"* Sometimes your athlete's disappointment might cause him to be unable to change his thinking in a positive direction. He might be pondering on his defeat! Change it immediately! Get him moving forward! If he cannot mention any form of success, bring it to the surface for him. Example: *"Do you believe you had some great first serves that worked today?"* Your job is to change the frame of mind your athlete might find himself in. Move to victory – away from defeat!

Your second question: *"What have you learned from this match?"* It is imperative that you give your athlete the first option to speak. Usually an athlete knows exactly what he has done wrong in a match. Instead of you (the coach or parent) saying what was wrong, it is far better that the athlete himself identify his mistakes. Our ability to identify and admit mistakes gives us a certain measure of control. Being told about our mistakes by someone else makes one feel inferior, guilty and condemned. A foolish coach will tell his athlete about all the mistakes he made. A wise coach will ask the athlete to tell him (the coach) about what he believes his mistakes were. Once the athlete has highlighted and reported the mistakes the coach moves to the solution! No issue! The lesson has been learned and you have to move on!

A possible third question would be: *"If you could do something differently next time – what would it be?"* The aim is to move past the mistakes and find solutions! Focussing on what was wrong makes us feel depressed and defeated. Speaking about the solutions for the future fills us with hope and anticipation to continue with the journey! If one result (losing) means the end of the journey, you have missed your mark as a coach! Success is not a result! Success is a journey, a way of living, a way of being...

Next question: *"If you could ask me a question right now – what will it be?"* The purpose of this question is to create an open mind-set! Usually (especially after defeat) an athlete tries to protect his self-esteem at all cost. Many athletes might find reasons for wrong decisions (in order to protect themselves). Once an athlete has a reason for failing or making a wrong decision – learning is impossible! Getting an athlete to ask you for your opinion, he displays an open mind-set without justification.

Very important – once your athlete ask you any question you have to understand that this is a crucial moment in building or breaking your athlete! If you highlight the mistakes you saw, you fill your athlete with fear of committing those mistakes again. It is useless and senseless to do it! On the other hand - If you come up with suggestions regarding fixing the mistakes (the athlete already highlighted), you will infuse your athlete with inspiration, desire and motivation. This is what we call – moving forward!

B) AFTER VICTORY:

Success is often people's biggest reason for failure! Success interpreted wrongly might cause an athlete to become arrogant, vain and over-confident. Many athletes have fallen from the podium because they stopped to focus on the small basic principles it took to get them there! To be successful is a much bigger responsibility than to fail. Once you succeed you become the target of the rest. Others will want to defeat you. In competition your opponents will "lift" their game because you are perceived as the champion. The onslaught of emotional energy on a champion is far more intense than for the average sportsperson!

After winning a match an athlete might be blinded because the outcome (winning) fogs his vision. Dealing with success is equally important to continue an athlete on a journey to success as it is after suffering a defeat. Success might cause you to be blind to:

o   The fact that your opponent was not the best

o   Small "cracks" regarding discipline, respect, humility

o   Fail to focus on specific skills you planned to execute before the match.

o   Your long-term goal (dream) by being caught-up in the success of the moment.

o   That success is a journey – not an event.

> *Success and failure is written in ice.*
> *And tomorrow the sun will shine...*

It is always a joyful moment after experiencing victory. It is important to celebrate it with proper humility and grace. NEVER celebrate a victory at the cost of the dignity of your opponent! Never belittle an opponent in celebrating a victory – even if the opponent was mean and unprincipled. The sweetest victory is when your opponent can share in it because you give honour and respect to him. This is true victory! This is what it is to be a true champion!

After victory the coaches' composure and energy is needed to determine the extent of the athlete's celebrations... We all have dreams. The dream in sport is to be the best of the best (world champion). If you are not there yet – celebrations needs to equal to the occasion. Missing it might cause you to be blown-up in your success... by a sudden defeat. Humility and respect is the foundation for authority. A true champion remains humble in his victories and he never seizes to show respect to the one he needed to master in order to become the champion.

Your first remark: *"Well done champion! This was awesome and I am proud of you! This is one of those moments we worked so hard for! I celebrate it with you!"*

Allow your athlete to live the moment. Let him laugh, share and celebrate. Let him talk to his friends. Let him share with his parents. Let him give out signatures. Let him smile and celebrate because the relief after such tension is amazing!

Once the moment has been lived properly, retreat to a quiet place. Congratulate your athlete again and then ask the following question:

First question: *"Why do you believe you managed to claim the victory?"* The purpose of the question is to get your athlete focussed on the basic principles it took to become successful (and to ground them once again).

The moment your athlete speaks, he hears himself (and sell himself) on exactly what he says! It is imperative for an athlete to identify and voice his strengths because you build on your strengths! If you feel that he can expand more, question him again. Hearing yourself confirming your own strengths is critical for building confidence for the future!

Second question: *"What do you believe happened to the opponent whilst playing you?"* The purpose of this question is to build mental capacity and mental strength. An athlete needs to understand that momentum in a match is dependent upon mental momentum! As we think... we are! Once an athlete can verbalise the defeating thoughts that might race through an opponent's head, he develops a confidence to be able to do it again in the future! As a matter of fact – he will be much more aware of the emotional energy during competition! Once you are aware, you can make better decisions!

Third question: *"What do you believe was the turning-point in the match?"* The purpose of this question is to develop a sense of awareness in your athlete to identify and utilize crucial moments in competition. Many athletes are unaware of these "critical moments" where the momentum of a match turned into the favour of one side. It is one of the most important aspects of coaching – teaching your athlete to identify and utilize critical moments to turn the momentum! There are really no right or wrong answers to this question. It is all about becoming aware of the existence of such moments and to identify them!

Forth question: *"If you could do something different or better next time – what would it be?"* The purpose of this question is to constantly stretch the thinking of your athlete. Once we become complacent, we become predictable. When you are predictable you are vulnerable. The aim is to constantly grow, become better and to remain unpredictable. Once you are predictable, opponents know how to prepare to beat you and sooner or later you will tumble.

Last question: *"What is your next goal? When do you want to start with it and how long do you plan to celebrate this victory?"* The purpose of this question is to bring your athlete back to the moment. Your athlete needs to understand that this is not the end of the journey! This victory is only part of the journey. Instead of living in the past – focus your attention on the future. End the celebrations and move on.

Every athlete is different. Some athletes have the capacity to understand the short-lived value of one victory. You don't have to worry about them. They can celebrate the moment and tomorrow they are back to the basics. Other athletes might get caught up in the hype of the moment and in the potential fame of the future. You need to ground them consciously in order to save them from themselves. I have witnessed many athletes who did not have the capacity to deal with success. Their success became their burden and their down-fall. They never developed the capacity to deal with success equal to the moment and the event.

As a coach – remember. Success is not an event! Success is a journey! It is a season in a person's life you share with him. The length of the season will be determined by his tenacity, professionalism, humility, capacity, physical ability, emotional strength, dignity and the amount of joy he experience in this whole journey! Make sure you fill each tank!

14.
DISCIPLINE – HOW IMPORTANT IS IT?

HOW DO YOU APPLY DISCIPLINE?

When we discuss discipline we will distinguish between the professional athlete and the school athlete.

SCHOOL ATHLETES:

One of the biggest paybacks of sport participation at school is the personal discipline children gain. Discipline is an essential ingredient of a truly successful life even though the world would like us to believe otherwise. It all depends upon what we believe success to be. To be significant in life where one impacts the world in a positive way to eventually make a positive difference in the lives of other people, discipline is an essential characteristic.

> *Discipline is defined as:*
> *Obedience to authority and orderly conduct.*

Our personal views regarding discipline vary, especially when thinking about school. Some people believe discipline robs children from their spontaneity and creativity. They view discipline as a negative action in a child's life.

Other people see discipline as an essential part of their child's upbringing. Right through God's Word His emphasis on disciplining a child (when he is young) cannot be missed (or even misinterpreted). Discipline is one of the characteristics God expect us to teach and apply in our daily lives. Obedience to authority and orderly conduct is non-negotiable. Obedience to authority is the foundation for personal leadership. You have authority only if you can submit to authority yourself! Submitting to authority (also an essential part of personal leadership) means that I submit to authority even when I don't agree with it (because of my personal discipline). The reward or consequence of such an act can never be underestimated! It is one of the first commands (going along with a promise) in God's Word: Exodus 20:12

> *"Honour your father and mother (even if you do not agree with them) so that you may live long in the land the Lord your God gives to you."*

Is discipline necessary? Without discipline you will die. You will die mentally and spiritually; the chances that you will die physically are also much higher! Discipline is the outstanding character trait of true champions and heroes. Without discipline a life will be characterised by rebellion, falseness, uncertainty and disaster. We are witness to it daily. In every newspaper, in every news bulletin and on the front pages we read the stories of mental, spiritual and physical death as the consequence of a lack of discipline.

Sport participation is a breeding ground for sound personal discipline (if guided and done correctly by a coach). However, when discipline is applied wrongly, sport participation might become the breeding ground for rebellion. We need wisdom for everything in life. Wisdom means that we know what to do with whom and when to do it!

The purpose of discipline and orderly conduct in society is to create a culture of effective education and learning where everyone has an equal opportunity to develop his or her potential. When someone acts in a disorderly way he robs another from that equal opportunity to develop his or her potential. The aim of discipline is in a large extent to prevent someone from robbing others from the opportunity of optimal development.

Traditionally, discipline is conducted in two ways:

a) Negative conditioning (punishment);
b) Positive conditioning (reward).

The true recipe for discipline is neither of the above. The true recipe for discipline is *self-discipline*. True discipline is not the consequence or responsibility of our educational system. True discipline is a character trait learned from birth as applied and expected by your parents or the people raising you. True discipline is what you learn from the day you are born.

When parents or guardians do not take responsibility for discipline in a child's life it becomes the unfair and unpleasant task of teachers and coaches to teach it to a child. This will always be a battle. If a person does not have self-discipline, a spirit of rebellion rises up the moment negative conditioning (punishment) is applied. A spirit of rebellion implies disrespect and violence (physical or mental). It is like a whirlpool of negativity which takes children from one battle to another. The educational system suffers because of this. Many children (and adults) are robbed of the opportunity to learn because of a lack of discipline in someone else!

When you try to motivate or change a child who does not have self-discipline (by means of positive conditioning / reward) it soon becomes a game of manipulation. Manipulation is a deadly cancer. You can only buy good behaviour for so long. When the going gets tough, true character (lack of self-discipline) will surface. Boundaries will constantly be moved. Eventually parents (and educators) are trapped by their own foolish effort to buy discipline.

Discipline goes hand-in-hand with responsibility. A sense of responsibility is essential for living a truly successful life. To be successful in coaching, discipline needs to be an integral part of the culture and your method of coaching. It has become one of the biggest challenges in modern-day school systems!

Many children are spoiled. Self-discipline is not a given and many children have become masters of manipulation. Parents are blinded and don't see (or want to see) their children's lack of self-discipline. By modern law any educator or coach is prohibited from using negative conditioning (punishment) to install discipline (especially at school level). It means that only those who possess self-discipline will eventually make it. The sad thing is that modern law (government) expect educators and coaches to successfully teach both people with self-discipline as well as those without it! It is an impossible task. People without self-discipline will forever rob those who do have self-discipline from the opportunity to learn.

WHAT DO WE DO WITH SCHOOL CHILDREN?

The traditional method in coaching children was:
Punishment / threats / aggression and anger.

Did it work? Of course it did – we've done it for ages! Was it effective? For sure – but only to a certain extent! Things constantly moved backwards. Consider the moral and ethical character changes of humans over the past decade. Did it get better and stronger? No it didn't! It got worse and society is getting sicker by the day.

Beside the fact that punishment is prohibited by law, the remaining methods of applying discipline i.e. threats, aggression and anger is probably the worst thing you can do in coaching children. Many coaches are conditioned to act with threats, anger or aggression. In such cases the true purpose of coaching is lost and it becomes a system where the focus falls on mistakes, (trying not to make them) threats, (trying to get some form of discipline) and fear (of making mistakes and losing).

Is THERE A BETTER METHOD?

For sure! We need to move the application and existence of discipline from the external source (coach or teacher or parent) to an internal source (self-discipline). When this happens, discipline is not a function of the coach or teacher, but a personal responsibility of the child or athlete. This form of discipline is the result of a verbal agreement the coach makes with his athlete before engaging in a relationship!

This method is simple:
What would you like to have from your athletes during a training session?

A	B
• A desire to work hard with intensity?	• Moan and groan when working hard?
• Being motivated and committed?	• Lazy and uncommitted at training sessions?

The answer is surely: Column A!

It makes sense! Every coach would love to coach athletes who love physical exercises. Physical exercises are the foundation of conditioning in any sport!

I want to ask: *"How can we expect children and athletes to love physical exercises if we use it as method of punishment?"*

It doesn't make sense! If we use physical exercises as punishment when children or athletes display a lack of commitment *we develop a negative association with physical exercise*. Children develop a mental resistance against physical exercises just as most children developed a mental resistance against reading (because they associate reading with schoolwork, exams and feelings of inadequacy and fear).

THE HUMAN BEING IS MOTIVATED IN TWO WAYS:
a) Avoidance of pain;
b) Search for pleasure.

Research has shown that we will always do more to avoid pain that we will do to search for pleasure. When we connect pain (punishment) to physical exercise, we will naturally do more to avoid physical exercise than we will do to find ways to engage in it. On the other hand, if we can get people to connect a pleasurable outcome to physical activity / exercise (e.g. health, movement, performance, fame, competition, accomplishments), we can actually get people to desire the opportunity to do physical exercise!

What connection do our children have with physical exercise? Is it perhaps:

?   Physical exercise is difficult and painful.

?   Physical exercise is a method of punishment.

?   I will always try do less rather than more - because if I can cheat it means I am outwitting my coach and I am showing the others to be fools.

What a tragedy!
How do we change it?

We need to change the emotional connection children have with physical exercise from pain to pleasure. ***To do this we can never use physical exercise as method of punishment!*** We want children to fall in love with physical activity.

Physical activity should be seen as an essential step in achieving your dreams. The moment you engage in a coaching relationship you become part of a team working together – NEVER working against each other! When one member of the relationship (the athlete) breaks the agreement (to work hard, be committed and stay positive), you (other member of the relationship) simply step back and remove the opportunity (physical training). It simply means that your athlete will not be able to live his dream any more (*the dream he sold to you in the agreement in the beginning*).

A condition for this method of discipline is that you and your athlete must have a clear agreement about the goal (your athlete's dream). *Your athlete's dream becomes the source and foundation of motivation!* Once this arrangement is in place, personal discipline is expected and part of the deal. A coach never has to threaten, quarrel and convince any athlete to do any physical exercise. Physical exercise is a privilege, planned by the coach and loved (and trusted) by the athlete! This is a win-win-relationship! This is a TEAM!

At school level the simple method of applying discipline is *to withhold the privilege of taking part in a physical activity / exercise from the athlete / child who lacks the self-discipline to allow others to fully benefit from the opportunity to enhance themselves.* Physical exercise needs to be seen as a privilege. A lack of discipline will result in an athlete being no longer welcome to take part in the physical exercise for that moment. It means he loses the opportunity to work towards his dream (for that specific session). He can only enjoy the privilege to train again once committing himself to the agreement. He can only be allowed to partake again at the next training session.

Doing it this way will cause athletes to view physical training as a reward and a privilege and not a dreadful activity where they try to cheat with every opportunity they get. It will transform your experience from cursing and threatening to a joyful adventure!

SENIOR ATHLETES:

Working with adults should never ever end in a session where power and threats are used to motivate them. Only a fool will believe that he can coach by means of threats, anger or aggression. Discipline with adults is simple – you agree before every training session on the principle of self-discipline. The moment self-discipline is lost (and other athletes lose out on an opportunity for high-intensity and quality training) an athlete will be asked to leave the field / place of training. If you want to cheat, rather leave. You need to create a culture of excellence, joy and high intensity during training. This culture needs to be clear and non-negotiable. If you dream to become the best, you train like the best! If you don't want to train that way, find yourself another coach.

Before every training session: Ask your athletes personally: *"How would you like to train this afternoon: high quality or average? Would you like me to expect high intensity from you or would you like me to make it easy for you?"* Every athlete needs to respond verbally. During training you only remind them (if necessary) about their agreement (have grace). By doing this you actually remind them about their dream (which is the source of their motivation)!

This method of discipline is exciting and totally different compared to the negative association we used to have with discipline! It brings out the best in every athlete – not the worst. Do it! It is different, but psychologically beneficial and powerful. The traditional method of discipline was mentally negative and troublesome. Once you experience the change of mind (and see the results) you will never go back!

FINDING THE DREAM (SOURCE OF MOTIVATION)

Coach: *"Victor, what is your dream?"*

Athlete: *"My dream is..., coach"*

Coach: *"What do you think we have to do to get you there?"*

Athlete: *"We will have to work hard coach. We will have to commit and master everything there is to master."*

Coach: *"I agree with you 100%. Can we make this agreement: This is your dream and I am a major part of your team! I will, however, never convince you to live your dream, you need to convince me! If you don't want to train with high intensity, tell me! It is your dream and I will work with you – never against you! Is that OK with you?"*

Athlete: *"It is 100% OK with me, coach"*

Now you have an agreement! All you have to do (when necessary) is to remind your athlete about it!

15.

HOW DO YOU COACH ATHLETES TO BECOME MENTALLY TOUGH?

Talent is an equalizer. Mental toughness and physical endurance is the differentiators! It is in situations of extreme pressure and high expectations where champions distinguish themselves from the rest.

How do you teach someone to become mentally tough? It is important to know that we are not born with this characteristic. Mental toughness is something we learn – it is a way of thinking!

Throughout this book you will grasp one theme: The relationship between a coach and an athlete is built upon an agreement! When two people agree on something, things start happening. In God's Word it is written:

> *Again, truly I tell you, that if two of you on earth agree on anything they ask for, it will be done for them. Matt 18:19*

As total coach you have to be much more than simply a technical expert, a physical conditioner or a strategic analyst. Your biggest role is to effectively deal with your athletes on a mental and emotional level. How often have we heard: *Everything is in the head*? When you plan to be a total coach you have to learn how to work effectively with your athletes on a psychological level. Mental toughness is probably the most discussed, yet least understood element of being a champion. The athlete who has the ability to remain calm in the face of disaster, who can keep his rhythm in the heat of the moment, who can remain in control of his emotions in the face of extreme provocation or disappointment, who can master the circumstances surrounding a competitive situation, who can deal with disappointment and injury in a masterful and superior way: this is the athlete who can be described as mentally tough. The question is: *How do you teach this to someone?*

It all starts with your dream. You have to see the end before you can start! Once the dream is clear you need to start sowing the seed for the future harvest. You sow seed by exposing your athlete (when he is mature enough) to every possible circumstance he will have to face on his journey towards reaching the top.

You have to know what to expect first! If you don't know, ask! Approach and ask the people who have walked the walk. Discuss all the different scenarios with your athlete. Look at success stories of others in different situations. Look at the mistakes others have made in similar situations. Plan a strategy and effective response for every possible situation. Decide (together) what the proper response in a situation should be. Then practice it! Simulate circumstances as far as possible in your daily training. Have an agreement with your athlete to do it. Your athlete needs to know that he will constantly be tested (trained) to make the correct decisions in the heat of the moment!

Very important: You need to get to a point where your athlete asks you to test / provoke him! ***Unless your athlete asks you, no mental shift has taken place***! Only once your athlete asks you to test (tempt) him does his mind shift into a pro-active mode instead of being re-active. Challenges will become a breeze to deal with when you train your athlete to master them. If there are circumstances in which your athlete is uncertain, he should ask: "*Coach, what do you suggest I do when this happens?*" Decide (together) by discussing the consequences of different reactions. **Simulate them** and let your athlete experience the feeling of dealing with challenges in a wise and mature manner. It always puts a smile on your athlete's face. It starts the adrenaline flowing knowing that a challenge is mastered!

Your athlete needs to ask you to apply these difficult / disruptive challenges (temptations) during a practise. If you initiate it (without your athlete asking) the first and instinctive reaction is usually the flight or fight reaction (negative). This reaction is precisely the mental conditioning you want to master! You master it by being prepared with mature and wise decisions instead of instinctive reactions. Wisdom in competition is to be prepared for any event and to be able to deal with it in an authoritative way instead of an instinctive way.

Once your athlete experiences victory by mental authority (wise decisions) he moves a step ahead (of his competitors). Being able to do it once is not an indication that you have mastered it! You have to be able to do it over and over again – eventually without being warned! Once wise and authoritative decisions happen naturally your athlete will smile in the face of intense pressure, negative spectators, disruptive opponents, provocation, etc. Your athlete will begin to understand what it means to be mentally tough!

THERE ARE **6** PHASES OF TEACHING YOUR ATHLETE MENTAL TOUGHNESS:

PHASE 1:

Ask your athlete to describe situations where he has 'lost it' mentally before. Explain the effect of mental pressure. Explain the consequences of wrong decisions and instinctive reactions in situations of pressure. Make a list of **mentally tough** situations that might arise during his career. Use examples of other athletes and the mistakes they made. Try to identify every possible challenge. Find some of the most ridiculous incidents that have happened in history. Prepare for the unexpected!

Once you have your 'toughness list' (possible challenges), discuss them with your athlete and find a wise solution (behaviour) for each situation. If you don't have a proper answer – find one! There is always a wise solution to every challenge.

> *Remember: You don't make a wise decision in the heat of the moment! You make a wise decision BEFORE the heat of the moment. When the moment appears, you are properly prepared. You are the master of the moment!*

Once you have the answers, you need to simulate them in order to feel them. You can only know what it feels like if you physically do it! Before a training session, remind your athletes that provocation and temptation should be part of any session. Sport and competition is far more than mastering a technique. It is about mastering all external factors influencing play. Ask your athlete whether he wants it to be part of his training session.

EXAMPLE:

Coach: *"If you want me to help you become mentally tough, you have to ask me to test you and provoke you. If you don't ask me, your natural instinct will kick in and you will probably get upset. We want to master instinct with wisdom. You need to ask me."*

Athlete: *"Coach, I want to become mentally tough. I want to master instinct with wisdom. Will you provoke me and test me during this training?*

The moment your athlete asks you to do this is the moment a mind-shift has taken place. This is victory over challenge! Start your training session. Whenever you see an opportunity to test / provoke your athlete, do so. Do those things you have written down on your toughness-list:

→ Try to shake your athlete with a negative remark.
→ Make unsettling comments like mean opponents will often do.
→ Try to get inside your athlete's head in a negative way.

Do this initially with a twinkle in the eye. Your athlete will surely check to see whether you are serious or whether this is part of the test. Once your athlete acts with wisdom and not with instinct, reward him verbally. Explain the demoralizing effect it has on an opponent when he doesn't fall for the temptation. Your athlete experiences immediate success – not necessarily in results (outcome), but in emotional control. Emotional control usually precedes a positive outcome on the scoreboard.

Summary of phase one:

a) A conscious decision to become mentally tough.

b) Make a *toughness list* to identify all possible challenges.

c) Decide on a plan of action for every situation.

d) Athlete asks the coach to provoke / test him.

e) Do it physically during training.

f) Give verbal reward for correct behaviour and discuss the effect such behaviour will have on the opponent (and yourself)!

PHASE 2:

✓ Ask your athlete to talk about his experience during the testing.

✓ Ask him to tell you what happened when he acted with wisdom instead of instinct?

✓ Ask your athlete to explain the consequences of these actions.

✓ Ask your athlete whether he can see the possibility of consistently acting this way in the future?

The purpose of asking your athlete is to get him to verbalise the positive results. When we speak and when we hear ourselves talk, we become convinced. It is far more powerful to speak these words ourselves than when someone else (a coach) speaks it. It is great when a coach tells his athlete what he believes has happened, but it is far better when an athlete starts to speak about the process himself! Getting your athletes to speak bring about an internal force of energy we call a self-fulfilling prophecy. It is a Biblical principle described in Proverbs 18:21

> *"Death and life are in the power of the tongue: and they that love it shall eat the fruit thereof."*

Getting your athlete to speak about the positive effects of mentally tough behaviour is the most important step of mastering mental toughness. Your athlete is now sold-out and he did it himself! This journey has just turned into a great adventure! Your athlete has started to grow his faith (belief)! Whatever you believe you will eventually prove to be true! The psychology of coaching is to get your athlete to believe in what he does. You want him to have confidence in his own signature act (unique ability). You want him to believe that what he does is working for him. The key is to get your athlete to speak about it himself!

The Biblical revelation behind this principle comes from Romans 10:17

> 'So, then faith (what one believes) comes by the hearing, and hearing (repetitive hearing) by the Word of God."

EXAMPLE:

"Janco, tell me what happened to you when you acted in this manner during training?" Janco verbalises how he played with confidence. He tells you how good it felt to be positive in the face of provocation.

"Tell me what you believe will happen to the opponent when you act in this way?" Janco sells himself on the negative emotions the opponent will experience.

"How would you like to handle this situation in the future, Janco?" Janco commits to become mentally tough. He verbalises the correct (wise) behaviour. He sells himself to you as to what you can expect from him in the future. This is how you build mental toughness!

PHASE 3:

Ask your athlete if he is ready to act with wisdom, even when you are not going to warn him? Provocation and temptation is going to be an integral part of training in the future. Mental toughness should become a habit, not an accident (mastery is never an accident). Warn your athlete that you are going to do more than just simulate situations yourself. You are going to ask outsiders and opponents (in friendly encounters) to consciously try to provoke him. You want to see if anyone can provoke anger, doubt, fear, irritation, surprise or meanness in your athlete. Mental toughness needs to move from a planned action into a life-long habit!

Imagine working with a rugby-team. Approach one of your players in private. Command him to deliberately make mistakes during a training session. Tell him to deliberately aggravate the rest of the team.

Before the training session ask the team: "*How would you like to train today? A quality session with high intensity or an average session and without passion?*" Every individual needs to commit to high quality and intensity. Make this agreement a routine commitment before every training session. Look at the reactions of the players once your "disruptive agent" starts to mess things up. Use your common sense!

o   If you see the players reacting negatively and irritated, stop the exercise and tell them immediately what you have observed. It is almost like moving back to phase two where you warn them about tempting them on purpose. Tell the players what you saw happening (negative vibe and irritation creeping in). Ask them whether they believe this is the best behaviour going forward? Ask them what they believe the finest behaviour will look like? They need to come up with solutions and they need to verbalise them!

It is imperative that you stop a negative training at that specific moment. Don't allow it to continue. Athletes have to become aware of their emotional level (mental toughness) at that moment. Show them that they can make a decision to deal with the situation in a different way!

o   When the situation is handled with wisdom (when the team remains positive and cover the "negative agent"), you need to stop the training after a while. Publicly expose and release the negative agent from his role. It will be met with great emotional release and fun. Reward the team verbally for their excellent behaviour and make them aware of what they did well. You can say something like: "The way you responded *showed me that you truly are a team of character and mental toughness*".

Hearing that they mastered the mental challenges creates the belief in them that they are mentally tough! Once we believe something – we will also prove it to be true!

> *Whatever we believe,*
> *we will prove to be true!*

Emotional control (mental toughness) is now starting to become part of the character of your team. Every individual is responsible for himself! Athletes understand that they have to think before they act! They are more aware of mental moments and they experience the consequences of wisdom in action!

PHASE 4:

Remind your athletes about their successes. Focus their attention on their masterful way of dealing with tough situations. Verbalise it when-ever it is appropriate. The aim is to make this belief (wise decisions) a habit. Once we believe we are mastering tough situations we will also prove it to be true. Instinct is turned around into wisdom and pride! Athletes need to be prepared for ANY circumstance with a positive and victorious mindset.

Physical fatigue is often the door to emotional weakness. In the presence of emotional pressure (high expectations), frustration and anger is far more likely to manifest in people's behaviour than during comfortable situations where people are physically fresh and mentally alert. In order to become a true master you have to master those difficult and fatigued moments. Create situations of extreme physical fatigue where wisdom in decision-making is far more challenging. Mental toughness becomes a habit the more you practise it in tough circumstances.

EXAMPLE

I have the privilege of working with my own children (mentally). I enjoy heightening my son's awareness of his capability to choose by asking this tempting question: *"Victor, am I getting in your head?"*

His answer to this (it is becoming a habit): *"You wish you could, dad! You know you are actually thinking about me... which means I am in your head! (Smile). I am doing great dad, thanks for asking! Nothing you do can get to me. I am having fun!"*

When he is physically exhausted and I notice that irritation is just underneath the surface, I will throw him a question like: *"What are you aware of at this moment, Vic?"* In this moment he understands that his choice of answer is extremely important! Instead of becoming irritated he needs to respond with something like: *"Everything is perfect dad – the longer we continue, the better I become. I love stretching myself to the limit. I know I will look back at this moment with pure satisfaction."*

PHASE 5:

Mentally tough emotions and decisions become part of competition situations. Traditionally people view competition with anxiety and uncertainty. Anxiety and uncertainty increase the mental pressure we experience dramatically. When an athlete experiences high levels of mental pressure the urge to act with instinct easily rises to the surface. We are often witness to top athletes who 'lose it' because of the pressure of a situation. In my mind I see a racquet being smashed in a moment of frustration, despair and anger.

The aim is to view competition with a feeling of excitement and confidence, not with anxiety and uncertainty. Excitement means that you have a burning desire to give it your best. You are ready to take risks and to discover the magic of the moment. Becoming mentally tough is greatly improved by accompanying physical actions associated with calmness and confidence. Athletes need to learn to physically act with confidence in the way they walk, talk and look.

Here are a few examples of physical actions enhancing mental toughness:

✓ A faint smile in the heat of the moment with a twinkle in the eye.

✓ Look up to heaven and verbally (and softly) thanking God for every opportunity.

✓ Show a "hidden" thumbs-up to your coach / parents in a split second of intense concentration.

✓ Bounce with vigour and energy during a break.

✓ Speak positively and with confidence to yourself during a break.

✓ Speak positively and powerfully after hitting a great shot (not in the face of the opponent, but in your own ears to uplift and enforce yourself).

✓ Constantly have a playful look of joy in your eyes.

✓ Smile with joy / fun even though you have just made a stupid mistake.

✓ Enjoy a moment of personal victory when you took a point.

To be focussed doesn't mean you have to shut down completely. Many people believe that they are focused when they show no emotion! Not necessarily! Even in the most intense moments of focus you need to channel your emotional energy towards joy and happiness instead of opening a door to fear and doubt. The ability to have a twinkle in the eye in the heat of the moment is what set true champions apart from *want-to-be* champions. Think about the likes of athletes like Richie McCaw, Rodger Federer, Novak Djokovic, Usain Bolt, Michael Jordan, Muhammad Ali, Jim Thorpe, etc. That twinkle in the eye is a characteristic the best sportsmen/women in the world truly understand.

PHASE 6:

Your athlete makes a conscious decision to become mentally tough. Before every practise your athlete needs to ask you: *"Coach, will you make it tough for me today, please? Bring on your best challenge."* It has nothing to do with arrogance. It is about believing in your ability in a moment of intense pressure. You need to learn to back yourself with the belief that your best is good enough. When an athlete becomes hungry to be mentally tough he will ask you (or anyone else) to consciously try to provoke / distract / disrupt / upset him in order for him to master the situation with calm wisdom.

It is this conscious request from your athletes that will indicate to you which of them are ready for the next step. The moment you ask someone as opposed to simply reacting to someone distracting you, your mindset jumped to a superior level. Without an athlete's conscious request, reaction is usually instinctive and not purposefully planned (trained). It is specifically this "planned wisdom" you have to apply to every part of your game!

EXAMPLE:

I once worked with the senior rugby team of a university. As usual, the reserves represent the opponents during a training session. The purpose of the reserves is to put the players under pressure whilst practising their moves. Watching them train, I noticed irritation creeping in. A few mistakes were made. They battled to get things right and the presence of the reserve (who obviously try to become a selected member of the team) increased the pressure (emotional pressure) in this situation. I heard a belittling remark. I saw a frown. The air was filled with an aura of negative energy. I saw doubt and uncertainty in the reserve as he backed-off to allow the team to get things right. Everything I saw was far more emotional than physical.

In our mental coaching session afterwards I asked: *"In your preparation for the next match, would you like to practice under perfect conditions where all your moves are performed fluently? Would you like to believe that you have mastered everything perfectly OR would you rather train under unfavourable conditions, high pressure and intense competition?"*

Their answer was clear: *"We would like to train under the most unfavourable conditions coach. We need to master any possible obstacles because we are surely going to face them in the games."*

I told them that I thought it was a wise choice. I then asked: *"Why is it that I see irritation and frustration creeping in once the reserves succeed in messing up only one or two of your moves? Why do you think the reserves feel hesitant to give their top-resistance during training? Do they perhaps fear being lashed at by the members in the team? Why is it that they apologise when they mess things up? Is any opponent going to apologise when he steps on your foot, mess up your play and upsets you? Unless you are prepared to deal with all this in a mature and authoritative way, you will always battle in the matches!*

You need to ask yourself: "What will it take for someone else to get into your head?" Your answer should be that **no-one and nothing** *will get into your head! If you doubt whether you can, you are a risk to our team. If someone can still upset and distract you, you are not mentally tough! It is one of the most important characteristics of this game: INTIMIDATION (getting in your opponent's head!). If you believe that you are able to do it, your opponents will believe the same!*

How do you think you are going to master this challenge? Do you think you can wait for every game to see what happens? Do you think we can practise it?

Imagine you **ask** *the reserve to do everything (within the rules) to provoke, disrupt, or unsettle you. Do you believe you will have a different mindset than some of you had during today's practise? When you* **ask** *someone to make it difficult, do you believe you will* *still lose your cool, get irritated and be frustrated? You won't! You know that you have to deal with it!"*

The team looked at me rather surprised. They never considered taking so much responsibility to literally ask someone to make it difficult! Imagine creating this culture: athletes looking and asking for the most difficult during practises, and then mastering it!

Imagine you (in your deepest level of spirituality) making this decision: To embrace every challenge you face in life instead of fighting it! To believe (in faith) that everything happening to you is happening for you - simply waiting for you to master it with wisdom! Imagine it becomes a conviction in your life. You will never fight, you will never worry, you will never fear, you will never stress, you will simply live an amazing life of exhilarating anticipation, thrilling excitement and true faith backed by your guts, determination, fearless efforts and willingness to prepare.

This is what competition is all about: bringing out the best in others and then to beat them on the score-board! Competition is far more than merely measuring talent against talent. True competition is that uncertainty of knowing exceptional skill is present, yet it is surrounded by mental challenges which will eventually cause talent and skill to be equalisers. The true master (of the mind and the skills) will eventually walk away with the victory. This is why the world can't stop watching those brave enough to enter the arena, a place of uncertainty, with only their beliefs, their experiences, their skills, their preparation and their faith as their armour.

16.

HOW DO YOU TEACH YOUR ATHLETES TO WIN?

It sounds ridiculous – why should we teach someone how to win?

To win is not as easy as we might believe it to be. We assume winning is similar to losing (not winning). To win is far more challenging than not to win! Many athletes don't know how to win! In life certain people rise to the occasion in the heat of the moment whilst others melt down in the heat of the moment. Society labelled this BMT (big match temperament). People with BMT are rare and special. They usually represent the champions amongst us. They possess that desired skill: big-match-temperament! BMT is a skill! A skill is something anyone can learn and master!

Winning is much more stressful for most people than not winning (losing). There are far more people used to (and comfortable) with *not winning* than there are people who really know how to win!

> *Winning is a habit. Unfortunately, so is losing.*
>
> - Vince Lombardi

Many coaches can testify to the amazing talent and abilities of the athletes they work with. Judged by their performances during practises or during training rounds, many athletes have the ability to compete with the best in the world. However, once the opportunity appears, their performances drop dramatically. The frustration and disappointment is an enormous source of stress. Many coaches can testify to the numerous talented athletes who could never win. They never developed their BMT!

Many athletes fear success because of the negative experiences they had as youth-champions. At primary school, the champions are the children who are gossiped about. The champions are put on a pedestal before they understand the responsibility of being a champion. Many of the youth-champions become arrogant, or this is what we all believe. Many of them simply built a wall to protect themselves from the merciless onslaught of pressure and expectations! Many of them never understood that it was not really their talent but only their rapid growth-curve that caused them to perform better than their peers.

Today the champions at primary school are more than likely:

a) The children with the wealthiest parents,

b) The children who have the fastest growing curve (early developers). They are bigger and stronger (at an early age) than their peers.

Early success (at primary school) is often accompanied by:

a) Tremendous pressure: parents and coaches believing they are the next world champion.

b) Arrogance: children who believe they are better than others because of their physical ability.

c) Bullying: other children tempting and provoking the champions to feel embarrassed about their performances. They are challenged to stand up for themselves and then the stories are spread that they are arrogant and spoiled.

How amazing to witness a young child who has superior ability combined with humility and gratitude! What a magnificent combination when children like this have parents who can be patient and wise in their support and guidance. Wisdom and patience is required to coach children like this to become true world champions. It is sad that this combination (humble child and wise parents) is so rare. Society has twisted success into a false image of fame, power and heroism instead of being a source of inspiration to others. Many children don't understand that early success is more than likely the result of early development rather than superior talent.

How stunning is it to see a child who understands this? To see a spirit of gratitude, confidence (not arrogance), respect and passion! It is admirable and inspiring. When a child like this appears on the scene people want him to succeed. We all want a humble spirit to succeed.

On the other hand, how sad is it to witness a youngster filled with arrogance, pride and disrespect. I have often been witness to this in my own life! We see many children teeming with natural talent walk on the court, yet no-one wish them to succeed. They have a mean streak in them. They don't lift others up - they provoke the worst in others. It is all about them. They constantly fight. When they lose they blame themselves instead of giving credit to an opponent. They easily feel sorry for themselves. When they win it is all about them and they often belittle the efforts of their opponents. Once they win a point they get in the face of their opponents with arrogance and provocation. You get a feeling of meanness and disgust when such a person walks on a court.

Many true champions (children) fear success because of people like this. What they really fear is that they (when they are successful) might become arrogant and prideful! Most of us know people who have a spirit of arrogance and selfish pride (a mean streak). We know that in our hearts we truly wish them to fail. This wish to fail is why many athletes avoid success (or the consequences thereof). Many children view success more of a threat than an attraction!

The highest trees catch the most wind. Successful people stand out. The average children are waiting for and expecting those children who stand out to fall. The emotional pressure accompanying success *at an early age* is constantly increasing (as sport and performance becomes more and more important in society). This pressure is the major reason for athlete burn-out!

What do children do with this pressure? If you have a talented child you surely wish him to have a healthy career. It is imperative to prepare your child in time to understand the pressure accompanying success. We have to coach these children to deal with this pressure in a proper manner. Many of these talented youngsters develop an arrogant image. It is not always because they are truly arrogant! It is often the only way to protect themselves from the ridicule and emotional challenges they receive from their peers. They have to arm themselves against the deliberate onslaught taking place - not only from their peers but also from the parents of their peers!

I work with numerous children on a daily basis. It is amazing to see how many shoot themselves in the foot (rather fail) because the pressure of success is unbearable. Success to youngsters means you will be labelled as arrogant, prideful and bitchy. Most children fear this label more than they desire to be successful. Success is not for *sissies*! You have to learn to interpret the emotional pressures correctly. You have to deal with the expectations of others in a mature way. You have to be able to withstand the physical onslaught from others with power – especially when you are still in primary school! You need to learn how to deal with these things in a mature way even though you are still a child. Your humility and gratitude should be unquestionable. This is a great challenge for any coach!

HOW DO YOU TEACH YOUR ATHLETES TO WIN?

STEP 1: YOUR ATHLETE HAS TO REALISE
THAT SUCCESS IS NEVER ABOUT THEM AS INDIVIDUAL – EVER!

It is very simple. Success is not about you! Success is about the whole team: your parents, your coach, and your opponents and most of all about your Creator! Through your performance God can be glorified and everyone else in your team can be proud! If you believe success is about you and that it is your own doing, you are arrogant and your success will be short-lived. You can only tumble! Winning a game or a match is only for a moment – then we are all equal again! If it is all about you, you can eventually just lose! No-one ever makes it to the top alone! We all need others and we all need a team.

> *Success and failure is written in ice.*
> *And tomorrow the sun will shine again.*

You have to understand that what you do, is about more than just you. You are part of a movement, a team of people, a message and a process of glorifying God. Your success is the result of the combination of a team. The team is part of a plan and the plan is about true victory in life! We can only have true victory when there are amazing challenges to face and master. Without challenges the victory disappears! You can only have true victory if you have a worthy opponent or a huge challenge. Without it there is no sense in effort.

Even if you don't believe in God, the principle remains the same. Success is never about you alone. Success is about everyone who shares this dream, the process and the work. You might be the athlete on the court, but others have put you there! Therefore it's your responsibility to share the victory. The more you share it, the bigger you yourself will become.

When you understand that the ultimate glory belongs to God, you'll have nothing to lose – you can only win! Once you start sharing the victory (with your coach, your parents, your opponents who gave you the opportunity to have victory, the officials who applied the rules, sponsors, spectators, etc.) you become a legend, a hero and a true champion.

Many champions' stories started in the midst of dreadful circumstances. Was it not for these circumstances they probably would never have become the champions they did. The key to their success was their circumstances and their choice to overcome them.

We might ask: "*Would they have done it if their circumstances were different?*" The answer is: "*Probably not!*" If we look at life this way we quickly realise that life is really not about us. Life is about much more than our comfort and our wealth. Life is about the victories we have over the challenges we face. Once we have the victory we also have a testimony! In our testimony lies our purpose because your testimony will give hope to the hopeless. Your testimony will show victory in the face of defeat. Your testimony will give glory to God if you choose so!

STEP 2: PREPARE YOUR ATHLETE FOR THE RESPONSIBILITY OF SUCCESS.

We all dream about glory and fame, but victory always comes with a price. Fame can never be kept personal – it will become public. Once your success makes you famous, and your story becomes public, you (your personal life) will become public property. Being public property is a massive responsibility. Your life is not about yourself anymore. You have more than just personal responsibility – you have an added public responsibility!

What you do, will influence others. How you walk, what you say, what you eat, how you act. Everything you do will be observed and most of it will be copied. It means (if you want to live a purposeful life) that you don't give yourself the luxury of being average anymore! Irresponsible behaviour won't be part of your life anymore. Your life will carry the weight of other people's dreams. You will stand accountable for much more than just yourself – you will stand accountable for thousands of others' choices!

Athletes need to understand this and be prepared for this. It all starts with the small things in life.

○ Respect towards authority - how you treat referees, parents and coaches.

○ Behaviour in negative circumstances - throwing tantrums.

○ Public conduct - how you treat others, how you greet others, giving speeches, dealing with media and reporters, telephone etiquette, social media, etc.

○ Your commitment in training - your attitude (others will watch you constantly).

○ Public image - neatness, dress-code and public conduct.

○ Sportsmanship – behaviour towards opponents, respect, disputes, etc.

○ Personal hygiene – your car, your body, small things of excellence.

I have a basic rule in my personal engagement with **athletes: *Wherever you go act as if there are people watching you, even when you think you are alone. You are always busy building a name – even if it is just with yourself! A good name is worth more than gold and silver*.**

It is necessary to give athletes guidance. There are fantastic research and basic rules regarding proper professional conduct. Most coaches don't know about the importance of these matters. Nobody ever taught them, so how could they know about them and how can they coach/ teach them?

MANY COACHES BATTLE WITH ISSUES REGARDING:

? Public conduct: Methods of communication, giving a talk in public, simple body-language principles, professional etiquette (how you answer a phone, writing an e-mail, introducing people, meeting people, etc.)

? Respect (foundation of authority): Some coaches are involved in a battle for importance with other coaches in the same sport. It causes them to belittle and degrade others with the impression that they are busy building a strong image themselves. It is deadly! You will only succeed in losing all respect and authority yourself!

? Behaviour during pressure situations: Some coaches lose it when things go bad. They complain about bad refereeing when the results were not in their athlete's favour. How can you ever expect an athlete to be mentally tough if the example you set is exactly the opposite?

? Commitment to excellence: Many coaches do not regard the small things as that important. For example: being on time, looking professional, talking with respect, being sharp, being physically healthy. Coaches need to become aware of opportunities to not work on technique only, but on mental toughness as well!

? Public image: Some coaches are overweight, undisciplined and give no care to their professional image. You can never expect anything from your athletes that you are not willing to do yourself!

We cannot accept (or assume) that these things are common sense. These aspects are extremely important. Authority is not something we get because of a position. Authority is a spirit you carry, born from the knowledge that what you are doing is excellent in every possible way.

CONVERSATION:

"Jaco, if it is your dream to become a true champion there are a number of things you need to get in place. Let me ask you: how do you answer your telephone?"

Jaco will be rather bedazzled because he never consciously thought about the way he answers his phone. There are principles at work in our lives. Principles are laws. We are not consciously aware of these laws. Being aware of these laws will give you a huge advantage because you can use all these laws to your favour without other people knowing about it!

Research has shown that the first words you say when answering a phone, do not register with the person who phoned you due to a 'scare-reaction' taking place. If you say your name first when answering your phone, the chances of the person phoning you hearing your name correctly are very slim. You want to be professional in the way you do things. You would want to answer your phone in the most professional and effective way.

The correct way to answer a phone is to say "Good morning / Good day" first and then you pronounce your name. For example: *"Good day. Jannie Putter speaking"*. You don't want people to need to ask: *"Excuse me. Who is speaking?"* This is not how you show respect and it does not create a professional image. It is actually unprofessional and rude to answer your phone with: *"Hallo"*. The person on the other side will have to ask: *"Who is speaking?"* Your opportunity to gain respect is lost. You need to understand that respect is the foundation of authority.

For every aspect outlined previously (public conduct, speaking, acting, etc.) there are basic principles (laws) at work. Knowing about them and applying them correctly will empower you. Mastering these things is an essential part of teaching an athlete how to win! It is all part of a winning mindset!

STEP 3: TEACH YOUR ATHLETE TO LEAD AND TO KEEP THE LEAD TO THE END:

What a frustration to see your athlete leading a match and then let it slip through his fingers. Just as he has to finish it off he starts defending and you can literally see the momentum in the game turn towards the opponent. You see how your athlete loses his confidence. You see how the confidence in the opponent grows. A dreadful moment in any match!

Your frustration rises moment after moment as you witness your athlete making the most elementary mistakes. Everything that has been done so perfectly up to this point is gone – as if it never existed! Your athlete becomes helpless and almost pathetic. The opponent comes back and wins the match to the great disappointment of your athlete and yourself!

The tears will probably flow accompanied by emotions of massive disappointment and intense frustration. he truth is: Your athlete did not know how to lead and then to win! How do you teach this to someone?

You have to practice the KILLER MINDSET. An athlete needs to learn how to think when he is in the lead. Your ability to win is often smothered and choked by a fear to lose. In any situation your focus will determine your direction. Wherever you focus – that is where your body will go! There are two major focus points...

a) You can focus on what you want to do.
b) You can focus on what you want to avoid.

As the match started, your athlete's focus was making the points, attacking the opponent and getting the momentum and score. Suddenly your athlete finds himself in a place where his goal is achieved – he is busy winning the match and he is in the lead! A small mistake, a missed opportunity and his focus can quickly turn. Suddenly he finds that he does everything in his power NOT to make another mistake. He plays not to lose (infinitely different from playing to win). He starts to defend. This is when you witness the turn-around in the match! This is the beginning of the end.

The answer: **Practise a mindset of pulling the trigger / making the kill.** Once you find yourself leading, you consciously learn to verbalise the words: *"Be patient, make the kill, pull the trigger, cut the throat"*. Your athlete has to practice to attack even when in the lead! Even when he makes mistakes. Even when the opponent has a few lucky breaks. Never back off, never panic and never doubt. You have done it up till now – it is all in you, just continue with what you have been doing up till now. Attack and play with wisdom. Be patient but persistent! Never let the pressure go. Keep the pressure. Play forward! The moment you step back is the moment when the opponent stands up and then the battle starts all over again. When the opponent is down, keep him down!

Make your athlete aware of what happens in the mind of the opponent. When you find yourself falling behind, you can either give up or you can attack! Most opponents will attack. When they attack they take bigger risks. Sometimes these risks bring reward (they work). If you change your strategy because of the *risk-attack-attitude* of your opponent, you will step back. When you change a winning strategy you are filled with doubt. When you doubt, you don't take risks, you don't follow through and you defend. It is fatal. Winning a match with this mindset is highly unlikely. Take risks, keep on attacking and follow through instead of backing-off. You can never play it safe in a high-pressure match and hope to win. The KEY is: *Secure the basics, then attack*!

> *Winning is far more difficult than mastering a skill... Why focus on winning if mastering the skill (the easier goal) will eventually cause you to win?*

It is about trust. Not trust in the outcome, but trust in your ability to do what you can with vigour and passion. You need to be sure that you have mastered the basics, because attack can only take place from a solid foundation of knowing and understanding the basic skills needed! If you do your best and the opponent succeeds in beating you on the score-board, learn the lesson and move on. It is part of competition and part of life.

Simulate situations during practice where your athlete is in front with only a couple of minutes left in the game. The goal is to continue attacking whilst maintaining control. You can't start to defend and prevent your opponent from scoring. Mentally it is two worlds apart.

Your athlete has to continue going for his shots, taking risks and following through. Once you see this happening, reward him verbally! The biggest mistake you can ever make is to teach your athletes to play it safe and to be conservative, especially when they are in the lead. If you focus on not making mistakes it is exactly where you are going – making the mistakes! (Read Proverbs 10:24 - The fear of the wicked will come upon him, and the desire of the righteous will be granted). It is a fool who doesn't want to make mistakes! A champion plays to win!

Your focus should be to make points, attack and win. Practise this mindset. When your athletes are mature enough and far enough in the process of becoming mentally tough, you can tempt them by making remarks like: *"Just don't make a mistake,"* or *"Watch out for missing your spot!"* Or *"Watch how I take this game from you."* Your athlete should learn to respond to this with a smile. If it is appropriate he can reply with a verbal remark like: *"Don't you worry, coach, watch me take the risk and watch what happens when it comes off. Why shall I fear – I only have faith and fun!"*

Very important: when you tempt your athlete he has to consciously celebrate any small success visibly. Celebrating success visibly (yet privately) usually upsets an opponent who wants to get in your head. Don't try to get in your opponent's face – it simply tells him he is actually getting to you. Surely celebrate any success with a fist-pump or a verbal booster to yourself!

STEP 4: TEACH YOUR ATHLETES TO STAY IN THE MATCH EVEN WHEN THEY ARE BEHIND!

To be behind is something most athletes dread. Perhaps it is because we fear it so much that it often happens! Unfortunately it is far more comfortable (less pressure) to be behind than it is to be in in the lead!

Athletes who have not been moulded through experience and hard work might easily give up when they find themselves falling behind. Tenacity (instinct to fight) needs to be developed. It needs to become a conscious effort to develop tenacity. You need to learn to fight with everything in you when you are behind. It is imperative to have a discussion with your athletes and you make it clear that becoming a champion is not determined by one match! Becoming a champion is determined by the development of character and tenacity in every match you play! It is (especially in the early days) not about the results, but the way in which you play which determines whether you move closer to becoming a champion or whether you move backwards to becoming a spectator.

All people look for security (sureness). We all avoid uncertainty at all cost! Children become more and more hesitant to engage in activities if they do not anticipate that they have a big chance of success. Children are not really afraid of losing. Their biggest fear is the ridicule they associate with losing. Ridicule and belittling by other children (emotional bullying) have increased dramatically. The increase of emotional illnesses amongst youth, i.e. depression, suicide, anxiety, anger, etc. is witness (and consequence) of this. This bullying is the reason why many talented young stars will never develop and mature in their gifting. Society is robbed from who they could have been because of their intense fear of the consequences of not winning.

The intensity of competition (winning at all cost) at primary school level has increased dramatically. The joy and the fun we used to see amongst primary school children are disappearing. We see more tears and more discontented parents. Sport has become an intense and serious matter. Young children are expected to behave and train like professionals. Their physical development is not the only victim in this process of chasing fame. Their emotional development is the biggest casualty! They may seem to be in control, yet the numerous tales of youth champions whose lives eventually fall apart is telling a different story.

Becoming a true champion is much more than mastering techniques and having the newest and latest technological equipment in your armour. Consistency in performance is far more important than being lucky and winning a match. True success is not a once-off experience. True success is a way of living, a way of thinking and a way of acting in spite of setbacks or challenges.

An athlete needs to learn to fight to the end, be back tomorrow and fight to the end again. This is how he develops character and pride. Once you have paid a price you don't let go very easy! When you get things easily, letting go is much easier too! Competition finds its true meaning and value in your ability to bring out the best in others. When you find that opponents lift their game when they play against you, you are becoming a champion! If you fear that you will lift an opponent's game, you are not ready to be the best yet! You should hope that an opponent lifts his game when he faces you! It is a compliment to a true champion, not an adversity!

Losers look for the easy opponents. They look for perfect conditions. They have excuses when they don't win. Losers think only about themselves. They can't give credit to an opponent who succeeded in outwitting them. They rather have an excuse instead of praise. Playing against a loser is never pleasant. A loser brings out the worst in others. A loser tries to upset, belittle, provoke or unsettle an opponent in order to beat him. A winner aims to bring out the best in another and then to defeat him!

> *The aim of a true champion is to bring out the best in his opponent, and then to beat him on the score-board. The aim of a loser is to beat the opponent on the score-board no matter what – even if it means that he has to belittle, hurt, upset and degrade his opponent. True greatness does not lie in winning. True greatness lies in conquering and mastering… with dignity and grace!*

When an athlete learns how to stay in the game, even when he is not in the lead, it is always difficult to beat him. If you succeed in getting the best out of your opponent, even when he is defeating you, you are never a loser. You are a champion! Teaching athletes to keep on fighting even when you are way behind is essential. It is not about how you start – it is about how you end! Simulate situations where your athlete is behind and instead of focussing on the outcome / result, focus everything on his persistent effort to stay in the fight. Never give up! Never quit on yourself!

A major reason why some athletes develop a loser's mentality (giving up when behind) is because they learned that quitting is an option when success is not guaranteed. Quitting is never an option! Once you lose belief (not in outcome but in your ability to perform at your best) you might as well not participate. A player without belief (hopeless, negative, without effort and energy) is a disgrace to any form of competition. Such a player is always the weak link in any team. No winning team can afford to have a weak link!

Hopes and belief are often awakened through the testimonies and the heroic achievements of people before us. Go on YouTube and watch the most inspiring videos of athletes who refused to give up in the face of defeat. Athletes who kept on giving their best even though they faced numerous match-points against them. By sheer willpower and faith they turned the game around and walked away with the victory. This is how legends are born. You need to tell your athletes these stories. You need to inspire them to do the same. They have to make a decision BEFORE the time: *"Quitting is never an option. I will fight to the end. Even though I may not win the match, I will make sure that my opponent will respect me because I never gave up!"* When you are young you might find that some opponents will ridicule you. They ridicule you because it gives them a sense of power in that moment. Even though they might belittle you in the moment, make them respect you in the way you play to the end! Build a good name. Build a legacy!

17.
VISUALISATION – AN INTEGRAL PART OF ANY SESSION!

WHAT IS VISUALISATION?

The definition of visualisation according to the Cambridge dictionary is: *To form a picture of someone or something in your mind in order to remember him, her or it.*

According to the Collins English dictionary, visualisation is *a technique involving focusing on positive mental images in order to achieve a particular goal.* There are a number of different definitions (opinions) as to what visualisation really is.

Visualisation is a mental action (or exercise) where you use your imagination to place yourself in a situation performing an action or seeing yourself react to something. In sport visualisation is a technique which is used with tremendous success to prepare the central nervous system (stimulation of certain muscle groups) to perform an action or task successfully.

Although many people might think that visualisation only involves the visual aspect of preparation, research has found that with practise we are able to involve all senses (smell, hear, feel, see, etc) through the act of visualisation. The more you practise visualisation, the more effective and meaningful it will become in preparing you for competition.

In her remarkable book,*Switch on your Brain* by Dr. Caroline Leaf, the author describes the amazing physical changes induced by visualisation. The physical body excrete endorphins through the act of imagining something which puts the body in a mode of action or preparation for action. She describes the amazing difference between the excretions of fear-endorphins (negative thoughts) opposed to the power of excreting power-endorphins (faith-filled thoughts). She also indicates that both these thinking processes have long-term effects on physical health.

Fear-endorphins act like poison to the body (makes you sick). Power-endorphins on the other hand act like energy to the body (enhances health as well as recovering). The most significant aspect about it is that we can control it by conscious choices we make! Research states the following positive consequences of visualisation:

✓ It enhances your physical performance.

✓ It enhances your endurance.

✓ It enhances your ability to focus in the heat of the moment.

✓ It heightens your levels of energy.

✓ It has a positive effect on the prevention of injuries.

✓ It has a positive effect on your motivational levels.

✓ It has a positive effect on the general feeling of joy you experience.

✓ It lowers your competition anxiety.

✓ It increases your ability to recover after an injury.

✓ It heightens your ability to gain back self-confidence after experiencing defeat or setbacks.

Competition is far more mental than physical. We have heard this saying more than once in our life-time: *"80% of the game is in your head (mental state of mind) and 20% is physical"*. Sports differ in its inherent character and the demands it places on athletes. There are sports where a tiny variation in a movement might mean the difference between winning and coming second. It's the athlete who is able to deal with circumstances in a mentally mature way that will eventually lead to victory. Talent is an equalizer. Mental toughness and physical endurance is the differentiator.

At the highest level of competition there is basically no differentiation amongst athletes regarding their equipment, their talent and their abilities. The real difference is determined by the mindset and the level of physical endurance of the athlete on the day.

In our search for more, better, further and faster, the mental side of the human being is little understood and even less utilized. Theory suggests that we utilise only about 3% of the human mind's capacity! The horizons cannot even be seen or imagined! We have so much to learn and so much to understand! Visualization is a fascinating part of illustrating and enjoying the tremendous power of our mind!

THE AIMS OF VISUALISATION

There are a number of different goals in visualisation:

→ Visualisation with the aim of mastering skills and techniques

→ Visualisation with the aim of increasing self-confidence

→ Visualisation with the aim to make better decisions in the heat of the moment.

→ Visualisation with the aim of managing activation and anxiety levels

→ Visualisation with the aim to have a high-intensity and quality training sessions.

→ Visualisation with the aim of creating a positive and tough mindset whilst recovering from injuries.

→ Visualisation with the aim of mastering moments of pressure (finals).

There are a number of situations we can prepare for by means of visualisation. When you look at the list above I want to ask: *"How much time do coaches set aside to make use of this extremely powerful method in preparing their athletes for competition?"* Is it perhaps an area we avoid because we are not 100% sure how to do it? Do we feel inadequate to apply and coach it? Are we a little embarrassed to believe in something we cannot see?

Visualisation is a simple technique. The more you do it, the better you become. You cannot leave this in the hands of your athletes. It is such an essential part of preparation. We will be fools not to use it! It will give you that edge we are all looking for!

HOW DO YOU DO VISUALISATION?

There is more than one method to do visualisation. It all depends on the physical situation; the athlete as well as the coach. There is no set time either – you can do it for as long as you wish to. It can be anything from a couple of seconds to half-an hour! You can do it anywhere. You can do it whilst standing, sitting or lying down – it doesn't matter! You can do it with your eyes open or you can do it with your eyes shut. Do it in the way it work best for you! The more you do it the better you will become. You can parctise visualisation in a quiet place or you can even do it amongst other athletes – even during competition! It is unique – just like you!

We need to teach our athletes how to do it! The more they do it, the greater the benefit will be. Visualisation is your ability to create a picture of an action or movement in your mind before the actual action has taken place. Some people are more comfortable doing visualisation than others. The reason is their upbringing and their personalities.

Some people are extremely realistic whilst others have no issue to embark on a "mind-walk".

Visualisation is a skill. Anyone can learn and master a skill. Some athletes will eventually involve more of their senses as they grow in their confidence and their ability to visualise. A skill is something anyone can master – if you really want you to! There are a number of guidelines to improve visualisation on various web-pages.

Visualisation is probably the most important preparation technique for any sport. Even in our modern era it is still vastly under-utilized and many coaches and athletes find it somewhat 'weird'. Some coaches may mention it but it is never an integral and formal part of their coaching. Do we perhaps fear the power of the mind? Are we afraid to feel ridiculous because we need to step into unconquered territory? Are we perhaps afraid that we might fail in doing it properly?

AN EXAMPLE OF VISUALISATION (A RUGBY COACHING SESSION):

Goal of the session: *Preparing for a successful and high-intensity training session*

> *"OK guys, let's get ready for this afternoon's session. Everyone flat on your back, hands next to your sides. Take a couple of nice and easy deep breaths and close your eyes."*

If you play soft relaxing music whilst doing this it enhances the relaxation of the body and the mind dramatically. The coach / facilitator speaks with a soft and gentle voice. Speak slowly and rhythmically.

> *"Feel how your body becomes heavy. Feel your ankles relaxing... feel your calves relax. Your knees, your thighs... your buttocks... your hips... your stomach... Feel your back almost touching the ground...*

213

Feel your chest relax, your shoulders, your arms, your fore-arms, your hands... Focus on your neck, your face and your mind...

I want you to picture yourself in today's training session. I want to see yourself on the field – look at your eyes, your energy-level and your intensity. See the passion and the drive with which you do things. Feel the adrenalin as you watch yourself. Imagine a bunch of kids standing next to your training field watching you with huge and excited eyes. See your reactions and how you perform. See how things work out as you planned. Others watch you and wish they can do it like you.

Take a deep breath. Feel the readiness in your body. When we finish today you will look back at the session with pride. Take a deep breath and say to yourself: "I am ready; I am going to do this excellent. This is great fun! We are champions!"

Take another deep breath. Exhale slowly and open your eyes. "Okay men, let's go!!!"

The total duration of such a visualisation exercise is about 3 to 5 minutes. These 3 to 5 minutes will double the value and the intensity of your training session! Why not?

My suggestion: Do it every day! Do it with every training session! Three to five minutes a day that will change your life! Make it a habit! Get over the strangeness of it and get comfortable with it!

It will obviously feel awkward and funny initially. It is new and strange! Amazing to see that the fear of taking the first step prevents most athletes from benefitting from tremendous value of visualisation! Before you start visualisation it is imperative that you understand how it works and see the value thereof. You have to want to do it. You have to believe in the power behind it! It is one of those easy to do things which is just as easy not to do!

THE PREPARATION CONVERSATION:

Coach: *"Do you believe that your mental preparation is just as, and even more important, than your physical preparation or do you believe that we should leave your mental preparation up to the moment?"*

Athletes: *"Coach, I know that mental preparation is extremely important, but how do I do it?"*

Coach: *"Have you ever heard about visualisation?"*

Athletes: *"Yes coach!"*

Coach: *"Can you do it and do you do it?"*

Athletes: *"I think so coach, but I am not sure."*

Coach: *"Visualisation is one of the most important methods of preparing your body for the physical demands of your sport. It is about your ability to mentally see yourself completing any action successfully. Research about the power of visualisation has shown that performances of athletes are significantly enhanced by making use of visualisation exercises. It has shown that visualisation is extremely powerful to assist you to:*

✓ *Make wise decisions under pressure*

✓ *Control your levels of anxiety*

✓ *Recover after injury*

✓ *Increase your self-confidence*

✓ *Take risks.*

We all know about it, yet we fail to make use of it! Would you like to learn more about visualisation? Do you believe we should incorporate it in our preparation?"

Athletes: *"Yes coach, I would love to learn more about it and I want us to incorporate it into our programme."*

Coach: *"Great! Let us start immediately. All of you lie on your backs. Close your eyes, arms next to your body and feet together. Take a deep breath. When you breathe imagine an orange balloon in your stomach. As you inhale, the balloon expands (in your stomach). As you exhale the balloon goes flat and the energy is flooding through your body. See the balloon in your imagination. Experience the relaxation in your body. Let's start at your feet: feel your ankles relax... your calves... your knees... your thighs... your hips... your buttocks. Feel how your stomach falls right through to your spine... Feel your chest relax, your shoulders... your arms, fore-arms and hands. Focus on your neck, you head and your face. Relax...*

Feel the energy filling you up every time you inhale. Look at yourself from the outside. Look at your eyes. See that twinkle of joy. See how you walk with purpose and with energy. See yourself greeting people and people greeting you back with respect and admiration. You are confident and your manners are appealing. See how your friends view you: with trust and respect. See yourself honouring your parents and the relationship of mutual respect between you. Feel the gratitude you have towards your parents for all the sacrifices and the effort they put into your life. See their joy as you thank them for it.

See yourself working hard at your academics. See the conversations of the teachers and their edification of who you are. See your disregards for the efforts of bullies to try and belittle you or to threaten you. See how your energy and confidence levels are always way too high for them to reach. You are ready to take action. You are ready to do things. You are alert for opportunities and you grab them. You walk in front. You sit in front. You speak up. You are responsive and awake. You feel good. You take responsibility. You go the extra mile. You enjoy your confidence and your humility.

See yourself training on your own, harder than anyone else. You know you are a strong link in any team, not only for your physical abilities but for the emotional energy and the encouragement you always carry with you. You love competition and you love the thrill of taking risks. You know that results can never change who you are! See the frustration and anxiety in opponent's eyes. They know you are a hard opponent. You are NEVER an easy match. You are always in control of your emotions. Your efforts are highly intense and extremely powerful. Opponents speak of you with respect and admiration. They use you as an example in their conversations.

You treat people with ease. You never take things too personal as you understand that all people are different. You are an easy friend, not a difficult one! You always carry a slight smile around your mouth.

Take a deep breath and feel the excitement filling you up as you see these things. Relax your body and tell yourself: I like this... This is my life... This is my adventure. These are my decisions... This is what I love to do. I am a born champion for God and He enjoys using me amongst people. It is not about me. It is all about glorifying my Creator. I am prepared, I am ready and I am powerful.

Slowly open your eyes. How do you feel? Is it not amazing? Could you sense how your body was ready to act and do exactly what you told him? Could you see the things I mentioned? This is just the beginning. It is going to get better all the time. Your ability to move into a situation will increase constantly. Are you ready?"

Athletes: *"Yes coach, this was magnificent!"*

Your athlete *bought in*. It is up to you to do this consistently and regularly - with every training session. If you let go because you believe you don't have the time or if you don't believe in the value of visualisation, rather never start! Starting with something (full of energy and belief) and then quitting it will cause your athletes to view any energised idea with distrust. If your athletes do not believe in you, you are busy with a lost case. It will never work! Your athletes need to trust and believe in whatever you do – in the same way as you believe and trust in what you do yourself! That is why it is important to do proper research and preparation (apply it on yourself first) before you sell it to your athletes!

Regarding the power of visualisation: don't doubt it for one minute. The scientific proof alone is amazing. Doing it yourself will change you, but you have to see it through! You have to create a "groove" through consistent repetition! If you want to become a total coach, visualisation has to be part of your daily routines. Disregarding it as a responsibility of your athlete is a huge mistake. Incorporating it and applying it daily will cause your athletes to enjoy a different level of trust and engagement in your coaching. Visualisation needs someone who is confident enough in himself to take other people on a "mind-walk". Become that person. You can only expect from others what you are willing to do yourself!

A THOUGHT:

Do you believe there is power and meaning behind the performance of the "Haka" of the New Zealand All Blacks rugby team? Do you know that they practise the "Haka" for hours on end to perform it with confidence and excellence? Do you believe they are ridiculous to get together in a room with huge mirrors to practise this to perfection? Do you believe they are stupid to spend so much time on something that's got nothing to do with rugby? Do you believe they are the best team in the world? For how many years? For how many decades? Do you think they care about what you think?

They are prepared to spend time and energy where others feel stupid and awkward. They make time for something like the "Haka" and we can only guess what else. What traditions do you have? What traditions can you create? Is the only tradition you have perhaps an old song that you sing together? What about creating something meaningful that can last? Not something you copy from someone else! Something original and something special! Can you make time for visualisation or are you stuck in methods of comfort and safety? Ponder upon it!

18.
SOCIAL MEDIA – BE ALERT!

It has come to stay. It is growing and the power behind it is astonishing! Millionaires are created overnight through the power of social media. People commit suicide because of it! It has become like a living organism in society. It captures our time. It sets trends. It forms opinions. It creates ideas. It can make you *and* it can break you. If you allow it to!

What a powerful feeling it is to know that you can influence and control a champion. All of us desire to be significant in some way. Significance is found in strange ways. We are all different and unique. It amazes me to see what makes people feel significant.

○ Some find significance in belonging to a group (a team or a gang)

○ Some find significance in rebellion (criminals, rioters)

○ Some find significance in saving the helpless (missionaries, social workers)

○ Some find significance in forming an opinion (trend-setters, designers etc.)

○ Some find significance in setting records (champions, magicians, freaks)

○ Some find significance in influencing others for the better (teachers, coaches)

○ Some find significance in influencing others for the worst (bullies, gossipers)

○ Some find significance in addiction (belonging to your addiction)

○ Some find significance in wealth (fools)

○ Some find significance in power (politicians, rulers)

○ Some find significance in performance (actors, performers)

○ Some find significance in providing (farmers, inventors)

○ Some find significance in fixing and building (developers, craftsmen)

○ Some find significance in surviving (tramps etc.)

○ Some find significance in defending others (soldiers)

○ Some find significance in saving others (life-savers, firemen)

○ Some find significance in destruction (rioters, gangs, criminals)

○ Most people find significance in sharing – knowing that there are others thinking like you do.

Social Media hit the button in the centre! Social media satisfies one of the major needs of the human being: belonging.

What do social media have to do with coaching? What do social media have to do with professional sport? Trust me – more and more every day!

This book is about the psychology behind coaching. Only a fool will disregard the power of social media over top-athletes. Social media has the power to make or break your athlete, if he allows or permits it to!

This act of selectiveness implies that we can choose. An athlete has to control what messages he receives through social media! How do you choose when it is too late? How can one choose if you have to read it first? That is the power of social media! It literally robs people from the power of selectiveness by taking away choice.

Except if we act with power greater than the power of social media (pressure)! When an athlete understands that social media has the power to poison his mind unconsciously, he might choose to use discipline-power to override social-power! This decision implies that someone else (a social-media filter) needs to select which messages comes through! This act of allowance is about an athlete's choice regarding what he reads or not! It is not about what we receive – it is about what we read!

A top-athlete cannot allow himself to read everything. Someone else (not the athlete) has to select what can be read without causing harm. You can't swallow poison and think you can spit it out. The moment you swallow it, it enters your biological system. It will kill you! You can't drink it and believe you have the power to eliminate it. It doesn't work that way!

Social media is extremely powerful. It can build people up (promote a positive image, use empowering words, etc.) BUT, it can break people too! Only one poisonous message sent by a fool who finds his significance in creating doubt can destroy an athlete's confidence! We are not immune to thoughts and words of doubt from whatever source. We are human! The solution to this challenge is found in Psalm 1:1

> *Blessed (happy, fortunate and to be envied) is the one who does not walk in the step with the wicked,or stand in the way that sinners take, or sit in the company of mockers.*

It is crystal clear: AVOID the traps! Don't think you can step into it and not get hurt! You can't believe that you can drink poison and not die! Avoid the steps of the wicked (the place where the wicked goes). Avoid the road where sinners walk (don't connect with them). Don't sit in the company of mockers (don't associate with people who have meaningless conversations). Don't think you can surf on social media and by luck avoid these people! They are everywhere! Especially on social media!

We live in a transparent world today. Every person around you has the potential to be as powerful as a journalist. Almost every person has a cell phone. Every cell-phone has a camera. The most harmless act or incident can be turned into the starkest mistake of someone's life. A harmless act (like dozing off in a class) can ruin your life! Press the wrong button and your (mistaken) opinion is sent into the universe where it can be read by anyone. You will be judged and condemned not by what you meant but by the wrong button you pressed! "Like" the wrong opinion and you will be discarded and thrown to the wolves. No matter who you are!

Athletes need to understand that their reputation is always on the line! Rumours spread like fire. One misinterpreted message might cause a serious movement of rage or anger.

Read the advice of a super-star who stepped into the trap of social media:

*"Read each tweet about 95 times before you send it. Look at every Instagram post about 95 times before you send it. **A reputation takes years and years and years to build, and it takes one press of a button to ruin**. Don't let that happen to you.*

You've done so much work. You've put in so much time, so much effort. Don't let one moment ruin your entire life because you wanted to be funny or you were mad or because you had a mood. Just be extremely smart about what you do. If you use it properly, you can do great things with social media. You can interact with your fans and have a lot of fun and share with the world what you're doing. But just be very smart about it."

If you have an athlete who is seriously considering becoming the best, he needs to be smart. He needs to decide to AVOID the traps of social media. Appoint a social-media filter. Find someone with enough common sense to delete any corrupt company from your athlete's social media list. Get someone who is able to identify poison and get rid of it in time. Find someone who stands in the gap on behalf of your athlete. A person who has enough clarity of mind to understand meaning behind messages. Get someone who has the wisdom to know what to avoid and what to allow. Appoint that person with great care. Appoint a person who pays attention to detail. Appoint a person who has the capacity to block any emotional or spiritual poison from filtering through to your athlete.

Be very careful what you comment on social media. After you press 'send' the world can quote you in and out of context. They mostly do it out of context. You don't need to reply to EVERY message. Least of all those that want to snare you through senseless arguments or opinions. Rather enclose yourself with more mystery than to be known to every fool! Let people think and talk about you instead of quoting you out of context.

It takes focussed effort, consistent repetition and hard work to build successful habits and faith. It only takes one sip of poison to ruin it all! When you decide to embark upon a journey of reaching the highest peak, you need to be willing to sacrifice popularity for the sake of respect. You can't please everyone. Best is to become a mysterious hero. People must speak about you with respectful admiration, yet little knowledge. Only a fool would want everyone to know what he does! Don't be a fool! Be wise and deal with social media with wisdom.

19.
THE FUTILE BATTLE
OF THE COACHES

The success of your life will one day be measured in how many people and things you have touched / built. Our sins are probably measured by how many people or things we have broken. Every one of us will one day stand in front of our Creator and give account of what we have built and what we have broken.

Being a coach means that you endeavour on a journey to build someone else in such a way that this person will stand out, be different, become more and be able to make a difference himself/ herself so that he / she will be influential and remembered by their children and their children's children.

You can't be seen as great if those around you are weak! You can never be a great coach if all the other coaches around you are pathetic! You can't walk proud believing you are a champion if the competition you had was mediocre. You can never be seen as truly great if those around you are truly small! The greatest of greats are those who can rise amongst the great. You can only be the best if you competed against the best. Once you degrade the abilities of another person in comparison to your own, you don't get better – you actually shrink to less of yourself. Never do it! Not even if the other person proves himself to be a fool! When you compare yourself to a fool, you will become a fool yourself!

I was recently approached by a coach to guide and assist him in building a solid and strong coaching academy. I have to admit, I was surprised. The tendency of most coaches (at any level) is to prove superiority, not reveal a need to learn and grow. This coach's academy was encircled by other academies within close range of his location. The competition for the best athletes and to outperform the other academies was intense. The atmosphere at the scene of competitions was intense, negative, unpleasant and mean. The parents felt compelled to join in this futile battle and so did the children. If you don't join into this battle your loyalty is questioned. Everything competition is about (bringing out the best in others) is challenged by this spirit.

The purpose of competition was totally defeated by this "battle between the coaches". The character of the sport and competition was mean, negative, disrupting and disappointing. In my conversation with this coach I immediately picked up an inclination for comparison. He habitually referred to the other academies' flaws. He pointed out what the other coaches were doing wrong. He tried to build a case upon the weaknesses of the other academies. His own academy was fairly successful, but not flourishing. He was having success, but once you measure your success in terms of comparing yourself to others you can never be truly successful. Success is far more than merely results on a score-board. Success is about making a positive difference in people's lives. Success is about hitting your mark as a representative of your Creator. Success is about having an indescribable peace within your being. Success is about your ability to live in harmony and peace with those around you, even fools.

I politely asked this coach whether he would give me permission to be straightforward and speak bluntly. He looked at me with surprise, yet agreed.

My words to him were: *"If you want to become the best, this is the last time you ever put down any other coach. No matter how good or bad he/she is! If you want to become great you can never be threatened by the performances of another. If you want to become the best you have to think like the best, act like the best and live like the best! You never look better by making someone else smaller. You never achieve greatness by robbing someone else of it. Greatness is achieved in the presence of the greatest. Success is measured by the strength of those around you. If you want to make your academy great, start by speaking favourable of the other academies around you. If someone asks you about the other academies you enlarge them, you boost them and you can encourage people to join them. If someone questions you in a sense to compare your academy with another say nothing about yourself, simply enlarge the other. Try this and see what happens."*

The coach looked at me with a question mark on his face, yet he committed to it. He started to enlarge and to enjoy the success of the other academies. Once he started doing this, something within him changed. Instead of being touchy he became easy-going. Instead of comparing himself (feeling inferior) he developed a spirit of pride (not arrogance) and authority. Instead of trying to prove himself he started to enlarge others. In only a couple of months there was a complete different buzz at his academy. People were cueing to get their children into his academy. The spirit of negative competition disappeared. A spirit of freedom and authority took over. Parents could relax. They didn't have to prove their loyalty by being mean or distant from the other academies' parents. Parents were encouraged to make friends. They were encouraged to set the standard of joy and excitement amongst the children. Clear guidelines as to the values and disciplines was set and agreed upon with both the athletes and parents. If you were not prepared to abide by these guidelines, you were encouraged to join another academy. Sometimes it is far better NOT to have certain athletes (and parents) as part of your academy. They will only ruin your good name! Instead of fighting with others, build with others! The stronger the competition, the stronger you need to be!

I don't want to elaborate too much on this subject as I believe anyone with common sense will understand the purpose of this chapter. You NEVER become great by putting someone else down! You never look good by robbing someone else from their goodness. You never gain strength by enlarging someone else's weakness. If you believe that, you are a fool indeed. Wisdom implicate that you never join in this futile battle of the coaches. Be the one that is different. Keep quiet, smile and focus on who you are and what you do. It is useless to focus on others hoping that you will increase! Let others join in their own battle for importance. Become the one that enlarge others. Become a mysterious hero...

20.

FOR THOSE OF YOU WHO ARE SERIOUS ABOUT BECOMING A TOTAL COACH

To be a total coach takes something special. Your focus can't be on recognition and the desire to become important. Coaching possesses a factor called delayed gratification. You first serve then recognition will follow! Who you are is more important than what you do! Just as Jesus' importance was never in doubt we know He was the perfect coach. He was a servant-leader! Your work is to find and unlock the best in others. In doing so you will become significant and important! Your value as coach is determined by your ability to understand and manage the vast amount of small, seemingly insignificant factors culminating into moulding true champions.

This closing chapter is a couple of short pointers to summarise the discussions in this book. Most of these pointers are "invisible skills". They are developed over time and through experience. Most of these invisible skills are often missed because they are not taught on normal coaching courses. These pointers are for you who are serious about becoming a total coach.

✓ **Make an effort to remember people's names** (especially your athlete's parent's names). There is a saying: *"A man's name to him* *is the sweetest sound in any language"*. If you understand what it means you also understand that you have the ability to make a very sweet sound in anybody's life!

✓ **Answering your phone in the correct manner** is your first way to build a good name (a good name is worth more than gold and silver). The correct way is: *"Good day, this is Jannie Putter (your name) speaking"*. By doing this you show respect (which is the foundation for authority). Answering your phone in a careless way will do you more harm than you can imagine.

✓ **Always end a written message with your name** – never (except if it is your wife) become so familiar that you disregard the power of respect. End every message with your name – it shows respect. For example: *"your message... Regards. Jannie (your name)"*. Small things make a big difference!

✓ **Always make sure that you have an agreement before your engage in a coaching relationship!** Without a proper agreement many relationships has gone sour and reputations have suffered as a result.

✓ **Avoid coaching (speaking) to your athletes with sun glasses on your eyes.** *"The eyes are the windows to your soul"*. Wearing sun glasses while coaching may cause you to miss the emotional connection with your athlete. Eye contact is one of the most important ways of building trust and commitment. When you are at a distance, feel free to put on your glasses, but the moment you get into close personal range, lift them! No coach has the luxury of becoming so familiar as to believe that eye-contact is no longer important or necessary. This is one of the major factors robbing many modern-day coaches from being significant and having true authority.

✓ **Answer any correspondence within a period of a day** (immediately is always the best). Administration is an essential part of any coaches' make-up. It shows your character, it shows your level of excellence and it shows what can be expected from you. You can only expect from others what you are willing to do yourself.

✓ **Give regular feedback to athletes' parents** (especially when working with children). It doesn't have to be a long report – it can only be a thought! Any contact shows that you respect the fact that you are working with what is extremely important in other people's lives (their children)! You can do it via cell phone message. Keep it personal (not bulk!) Even though you might send out a similar message to all the parents, make sure that you start your message with their names!

✓ **Be neat and professional at all times.** Familiarity is the deadliest trap for any relationship, especially in coaching! Even though you might be working with your own children, be proud of the way you do things!

✓ **Be disciplined in your own life!** Make sure that you take care of your own personal relationships (your wife or girlfriend) and never sacrifice what is important to you at the cost of your coaching. Some coaches try to manipulate their athletes through guilt (by implying that if he is willing to sacrifice relationships and put the game first, so should the athlete). Guilt should never be used for motivation. It is lethal!

✓ **Keep the fun in coaching!** The moment you become so serious that joy is lost you will also lose the hearts of your athletes.

✓ **Be on time!** Respect for other people's time is essential in creating trust and safety. If you don't value time, you don't value other people. If you don't value others you can never be truly successful.

✓ **Keep to your word / agreement.** The fastest way of losing authority is allowing yourself the luxuries of mediocrity, yet expecting a high level of excellence from your athletes. It doesn't work that way!

✓ **Greet your athletes personally** – before and after training sessions! The more effort you make to engage personally, the more respect and trust you will receive back. Any relationship based on respect is amazing!

✓ **If possible, greet the parents of your athletes with a handshake – every time!** The respect and loyalty will return to you! Parents will cover you when anyone wants to say something bad about you. You will receive what you give (and so much more!). You can't ever be too busy to give people recognition by greeting them personally.

✓ **Be prepared for sessions.** Before training you have to tell your athletes what they are going to do. You need to tell them the purpose of the exercises and how it will benefit them. Preparedness brings discipline and professionalism to the table. It will contribute to your good name.

✓ **Before every training session** make a verbal agreement with every athlete as to what can be expected from him during the training.

✓ **Make visualisation part of training.** Visualisation is a powerful coaching tool used by few coaches. It is available, it costs nothing and it will produce amazing fruits!

✓ **Make sure that excellence is part of your set-up!** Never settle for anything average. Take care of the small stuff (state of your equipment / cleanliness of your environment, etc.). Nothing ruins a good name quicker than an average set-up when excellence is available!

✓ **When you make mistakes, apologise publicly (in front of your other athletes).** It sets a standard of excellence and prevents anyone from spreading a rumour which will ruin your good name. Never be too important and too mean to believe you are above making mistakes. If you do not allow yourself to make mistakes and acknowledge them, your athletes might easily develop a fear of failure themselves.

✓ **Make use of humour in our coaching.** Humour is a special skill which when applied with wisdom and in the proper manner will cause your athletes to relax and not take everything personal. Healthy humour is a sign of emotional intelligence and maturity. Not all athletes may be comfortable with it (as many people come from serious homes). Regarding this culture of humour, never adapt to your athletes, they adapt to you! Teach your athletes the power of humour. If you don't have humour, find some!

Humour can change momentum in the heat of a moment. Most athletes believe they have to be hard on themselves all the time. They tend to take critique and correction too serious. Know your athletes and show them the power of humour. Appropriate humour has a fine line. Immature athletes might abuse the use of humour and move to familiarity. Humour is a skill you need to practice and apply with wisdom! Humour is a sign of authority and freedom of spirit. An insecure coach will be threatened by the use of humour. Such a coach's' authority doesn't come from his person but from his position. Ask yourself: Are you threatened by humour or are you comfortable with it? Humour is a magnificent tool available to every mature and total coach!

✓ **Give personal attention (and eye-contact) to any athlete looking for it.** When an athlete cannot see that it is not convenient for you to speak to him, put your hand on his arm (get his attention) and say: *"Fanie, I would love to hear what you say, but I have to continue right now. Can we discuss this after training?"* After training, make sure to call on that athlete. You say: *"Fanie, I have another meeting at 6pm, but I would love to hear what you have to say... can you tell me quickly?"* (Have an open a door to leave at a certain time for certain people love to keep your attention).

✓ **Smile regularly.** I see many (too many) coaches who always look concerned and serious. Relax! Your athletes learn to mimic your levels of emotional intensity. Build a healthy balance between focus and fun. Being too critical will cause your athletes to develop a fear of failure. You will have athletes who constantly play it safe. You don't want "safe" athletes! You want courageous athletes! Athletes who are willing to take risks without condemning themselves when things don't work. A smile with a wink of the eye can change the world!

✓ **Coach with stories.** A clever coach will understand the power of creating lasting and exciting pictures in the minds of his athletes by telling stories. Instead of telling it as a theory, tell it through a story. It will be part of your legacy!

✓ **Make sure that your athlete understand the power (and dangers) of social media!** You need to educate your athletes regarding social communication and the influence it might have on their lives. Rather be a mystery than being labelled as a fool. Be sure that anything you say can and will be distorted into a storm that might ruin your reputation! Have wisdom.

✓ **Never ever join in the foolish battle of the coaches.** Enlarge others. Edify other coaches and support them – you will eventually have more and better athletes and amazing parents!

FINAL THOUGHT...

What makes a sunset beautiful? Our ability to see it, but more so our ability to share what we see with someone else!

What makes life beautiful and thrilling? Is it the comfort and wealth we create or is it perhaps the memories we treasure and the victories we have experienced? In life we need to find what's possible, what's amazing and what's beautiful.

As coach you take someone else on a journey. You will risk many things in unlocking the potential of another person. Mistakes and disappointments will be part of this journey. Mistakes are part of being human. Instead of dreading it and avoiding it, embrace it and learn from it! It makes us all better. Experience ensures that we can be back tomorrow and be better. The aim of competition is to bring out the best in others... and then beat them!

Coaching is an amazing journey. It can take you places others can only dream of. You can be the host in someone else's life taking him or her or them on the adventure of a lifetime. To become a total coach is a unique and special experience available to those of you who are willing to risk ridicule, failure, success and... yourself. I have been doing this for more than twenty years. I love every moment. It is truly a thrilling adventure!

I am eager to one day hear: *"Well done, my special servant, you have made a difference!"* What are you going to hear? Go for it – why not?

I trust that we will meet one day!

Yours truly
Jannie Putter

CATALOGUE

A personal story about the challenges I had to face and questions I had to ask in my own life – going off-track, blaming circumstances, feeling sorry for myself. Questions regarding authority, rebellion, pornography (addiction), disappointments in people etc....and choosing to live a life of victory – not defeat!

Discussing twenty key factors that need to be mastered in order to become mentally tough in competition and in life.

A book about raising children and facing the challenges of modern-day living. Single parenthood, building a strong self-image, dealing with bullying, a system where we are so easily labelled with an attention-disorder... Building a healthy family!

Various CD's available to order from my web-site and down-loadable on your computer. Go to www.jannieputter.co.za

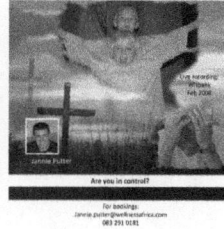

WORKSHOPS

Arrange and book a workshop in your town or school on:

- Parenting
- Coaching
- Teamwork
- Leadership

E-mail: jannie@jannieputter.co.za

www.ingramcontent.com/pod-product-compliance
Lightning Source LLC
LaVergne TN
LVHW041213080426
835508LV00011B/942